A German Stargazer's Book of Astrology
(Astronomia Teutsch Astronomei 1545)

A German Stargazer's Book of Astrology
(Astronomia Teutsch Astronomei 1545)

Translated and edited by Peter Stockinger

Foreword by Sue Ward

Mandrake

© Peter Stockinger & Mandrake 2014
First Edition

All rights reserved. No part of this work may be reproduced, stored in a retrieval system, or transmitted in any form or by any means, electronic, mechanical, photocopying, recording or otherwise without the prior permission of the publisher.

Contents

Foreword 9
Introduction 12
A German Stargazer's Book of Astrology 50
(Astronomia Teutsch Astronomei 1545) 50
Preamble 50
Of the Nine Spheres of Heaven 51

Part One SIGNS and IMAGES 54
Of the Nine Spheres of Heaven 54
Of the Twelve Heavenly Signs / and why they are named thus 54
Of the Twelve Signs their Stars and Effects 57
Sphere of the Twelve Signs and their Nature 70
Characters and Figures of the Aspects 70
Contrafacture and Pictures of the Heavenly Bodies / with the Fixed Stars 72
Images / Heavenly Pictures 72
Of the Fixed Stars and their Qualities 73

Part Two PLANETS 99
Of the Seven Planets 99
Of the Order / Manners and Properties of the Planets 99
Of the Complexion of the Twelve Signs and the Planets 107
Of the Dignities of Planets 112
Of the Joy of Planets 113
Of the Fall of Planets 113
Masculine and Feminine Planets and Signs 113
The Characteristics of the Planets 114
Of [the] Aspect or Sight of the Planets 114
Of [the] Significance of Aspects 115
Of Strength and Weakness of the Planets 116
Of the Beginning of the Year / how one has to take heed /
wherein Planets and Signs the Sun or the Moon will enter /
and to judge accordingly 116
Of the Lord of the Year 116
Of the Significance of the Lords and Houses 119
Of Dignity and Elevation of one Planet Above the Other / and its meaning .. 123

    Of the Conjunctions of the Planets and their Meaning 126
    Of the Strength of the Planets 134

Part Three MUNDANE ASTROLOGY 136
    Of Eclipses. 136
    Rules and Indications to Judge Eclipses 136
    The Meaning of Eclipses 138
    Of Comets 141
    The Interpretation of Comets in Every Sign / and Angle of Heaven 141
    Rules and Instructions / to Judge Comets and their Effects 149
    How One Should Recognize the Effect[s] of Comets 155
    Of Shape / Size / Complexion / Colour / Nature and Significance /
    of each Comet 160

Part Four WEATHER 166
    Of Nature / and Ways of Times / and Movement of the Sun 166
    Of the Four Seasons of the Year 168
    Dignities of the Signs 169
    Another Useful Tractate and Chapter / of Nature / Virtue and Effect / of the
    Twelve Signs 170
    Of the Influence of Planets / another useful chapter 172
    Of the Darkness / Brightness / and Colour of the Planets /
    and their Meanings / in the Change of the Air 175
    The Twelve Centers of the Moon 178
    Of the Opening of the Planetary Portals 179
    The four Seasons and their Properties 179

Part Five PERPETUAL CALENDAR 180
    Claudius Ptolemy / Of Rising and Setting / Significance and Influence / of the
    Changes in the Sky / Throughout the Year / Every Day /
    the Heavenly Pictures / and their Stars. 180

Part Six ASTRONOMY 207
    Explanation of the Spheres 207
    Explanation of the Spheres and Circles of Heaven 207
    Another Explanation of the Spheres and Circles of Heaven 209
    Meaning and Height of the Spheres 214
    Size of the Planets above the Earth 215
    Size of the Fixed Stars 216
    The Eighth Heaven 217
    Of the Epicycle 220

Of the Movement of the Planets against the Firmament 219
Of the four Parts of Heaven 221
Of the Movement of the Heavens and Planets 222
The seven Climates 224
Sphere of the Winds 227
The four Regions or Heavens 227

Appendix A 229
Appendix B 232

Foreword

Since the 1980s and probably more so than at any other period in recent times, there has been a rapid growth of interest in the written evidence of ancient occult practises, astrology being prominent among them. Practitioners and some scholars have been instrumental in locating previously obscure manuscripts and publications and some have been translated into modern languages. For large numbers of astrologers, the greatest step forward in this regard was the re-publication, in 1985, of *Christian Astrology* by William Lilly. First published in 1647, it represents the first book of its kind to be published in English. As a primer it is second to none and it was received by astrologers with great excitement which led to an upsurge of interest into, what has become known as, "traditional astrology". Lilly's work itself marked a turning point and many of the books which followed his, were copies varying only by degree. He had gathered together a very large collection of books about astrology, most printed in previous centuries, for example Abu Mashar, Galen and Cardan to name just a very few. His study and research enabled him to collate the information found therein – as was the normal practise at that time - into one book adding his own practical examples. However, this revival was short-lived and by the end of the 17th century interest in astrology was waning and the educated classes moved on with what is generally referred to as the Enlightenment.

Later in the 20th century, texts from the medieval "Arabic" period were translated and published and 'medieval astrology' was born. This period actually relates generally to the "Moorish" occupation of the Iberian Peninsula, some of the better known authors of that time being Jewish rather than Arab, for example ibn Ezra, Masha Allah and Sahl. Iberia had become home to many great scholars from a variety of religious backgrounds, but, with the restitution of the Christian kings, "The Reconquista", over time life for the Jews became very uncomfortable. This culminated with the last notable expulsion which closed the 16th century and here we find a close connection with the evolution of astrological knowledge.

The exiled scholars were welcomed by some of the principalities of northern Europe and the proliferation of "Arab" texts was continued by the scholars of that part of the world. At each stage, scholars attempted to reconstitute the body of knowledge belonging to their predecessors. In trying to understand that knowledge and extrapolate from it, they continued a long tradition among esotericists and we see exactly that later with William Lilly's work. We also see it in the present translation: that gathering together of much older texts and writings in order to present the work again from a more modern perspective.

In terms of research in our present age, little has been done relating to the period and location of this translation, and yet it represents an important connection between the medieval and early modern periods as far as astrology is concerned. As Iberia was to occult study in the earlier period, so Bavaria and Bohemia became in the later period, particularly the 16th century. This transitional period still has not been researched to the same depth as have the periods relating to medieval and traditional astrology and so we have a hiatus in our knowledge of the evolution of astrological and other esoteric knowledge.

In Europe, the influence of the humanists during the time of the Protestant Reformation of the 16th century, combined with the possibilities of large-scale printing, changed the views of scholars and educated people of middle rank. Scholastic views, which had been so important throughout medieval times, were now questioned, resulting in a review of traditional textbooks and sources. It is highly likely that the original Arab source material upon which medieval astrology was based was scrutinised in a similar manner. At the same time the demand for printed books, published in the vernacular, was increasing. All of these developments resulted in astrological textbooks being published in the native tongue of the author.

An obvious omission in this book is the lack of any reference to horary, the astrology of interrogations, categorised as judicial astrology along with the judgement of nativities and other subjects. It is to this that the Church objected. Natural astrology, which deals with astronomical phenomena such as comets and eclipses, was accepted because it sought to interpret the Will of God not to usurp it as was suspected with judicial astrology.

A German Stargazer's Book of Astrology is an excellent and early example of the popularity of astrology during the 16th century. Its style is didactic and generally informative requiring a lower educational standard of the reader than would otherwise have been the case. By publishing in German, the author predates William Lilly by over a century and it is clear from the latter's bibliography in *Christian Astrology* that he owed much to similar authors of northern Europe. Authors like Garcaeus, Gauricus, Naibod, Stoeffler and Schöner have been generally underestimated and overlooked by astrologers. With his first class translation of the present work, Peter Stockinger has begun to correct such omissions and made it possible for the reader to add another piece to this intriguing jigsaw. With its translation kept very close to the format and style of the original text, *Astronomia Teutsch* provides the reader with an insight into the mind of the 16th century astrologer and begins to build a bridge between the astrologers of the late medieval and early modern periods.

Sue Ward

Introduction

Astronomia Teutsch presents a milestone in the history of astrological texts even though it has never been republished since its first printing in 1545. Now, after more than 450 years, this new translation allows the English reader access to this rare work, providing a glimpse into the way in which 16th century astrology and astronomy were practiced in Europe.

Much of the source material used in *Astronomia Teutsch* stems from Arabic texts and we know that the transmission of Arab and Persian astrology took place from as early as the middle of the 12th century. John of Seville, (to name only one of the early scholars dedicated to the survival of original source material), translated the works of famous astrologers like Alkindi, Albumasar, Messahala or Thebit ibn Qurra directly from the Arabic into Latin. Nevertheless it would take until the 16th century for the first astrological works to be printed and published in the vernacular: Stoeffler and Pflaum published their *Almanach Teutsch* (German Almanac) in 1510 and Regiomontanus published his *Kalendarius Teutsch Maister Joannis Küngspergers* (Master Johannes Königsberger's German Calendar) in 1512. Yet these were only almanacs and calendars, albeit including prognostications for the coming year.

It was another 40 years before one of the earliest astrological textbooks in German, *Astronomia Teutsch Astronomei*, was printed. It was published in Frankfurt am Main in 1545 by Enriaco Jakob zu Bath. One can only speculate about the authors and the origin of the old, handwritten book, but it has to be noted that what we are witnessing here is the transformation of one single handwritten collection of manuscripts into a printed, and therefore mass produced, astrological textbook. The fact that it was written in the vernacular increased accessibility for interested readers even further. Contrary to German readers, the British students of astrology would have to wait another one hundred years for this to happen when William Lilly published his textbook *Christian Astrology* in 1647.

The importance of the publication of *Astronomia Teutsch Astronomei* can be judged by the fact that as early as 1569 Nicolaus Rensberger had copied several of its chapters into his own textbook *Astronomia Teutsch* (German Astrology), and in 1592 a book called *Astronomia Teutsch Himmels Lauff* (German Astrology's Heavenly Movement) was published which included portions of the original text. Because *Astronomia Teutsch Astronomei* can be seen as a landmark in the history of astrology, I decided to translate it into English. In this way, I hope that a re-publication of this book will enable the reader to compare its textual content with recently published textbooks translated from the Latin which were translated directly from the Arabic, and to provide the possibility of learning more about the transmission of astrological lore in the post-Arab period.

Although *Astronomia Teutsch* does not include a bibliography, its authors mention the names of several authors and some of their publications throughout the text. In the following I provide some information about these authors and their work relevant to the text.

Hali Abenragel. Abû l-Hasan 'Alî ibn Abî l-Rijâl (also known as Haly, Hali or Albohazen Haly filii Abenragel) was an Arab astrologer who lived between the end of the 10th and the first half of the 11th century. He is mentioned under his full name of Hali Abenragel in the chapter *Rules and Instructions to Judge Comets,* and as Hali in other chapters. Although we cannot be sure that the author is referring to the same Hali, it is very likely. Haly Abenragel's book was translated into Old Castilian and this manuscript was translated into Latin and first printed by Erhard Ratold at Venice in 1485 under the title *Praeclarissimus liber completus in judiciis astrorum* ("The very famous complete book on the judgement of the stars"), commonly known as *De iudiciis astrorum.* Subsequent editions of this popular work were published in 1503, 1520, 1523, 1525, 1551 and 1571.

Albumasar. Abu Ma'shar al-Balkhi, (also known in the Latin West as Albubaxar, al-Falaki, Apomasar Abalachi or Ibn Balkhi) born 787 in the Persian province of Balkh, was a Persian astrologer, astronomer and mathematician. It is said that his work introduced the philosophy of Aristotle into the Western World. Albumasar was probably one of the most influential authorities on astrology in medieval and Renaissance Europe. He wrote about forty treatises, several of which were translated into Latin from the twelfth century onwards. The chapter *Of the Lord of the Year* draws heavily on Albumasar's *Book of Revolutions of the World-Years*. This work was translated into Latin by John of Seville under the title *Flores* in the 12th century. It was printed by Erhard Ratold at Augsburg in 1488, 1489 and 1495 and by the house of Sessa in Venice in 1488 and 1506. David Pingree suggests that Flores is identical with *De revolutionibus annorum mundi seu liber experimentorum*, which has also been translated by John of Seville.[1] This work is mentioned, together with what is called Abumashar's "Book of Conjunction" in the section about comets. This work, with the correct title *Book of Conjunctions*, was translated by John of Seville and the translation was printed by Erhard Ratold at Augsburg in 1489. There was also a reprint by Jacobus Pentius de Leucho at Venice in 1515.[2]

Alfraganus. Al-Farghānī, Abu'l-'Abbās Aḥmad Ibn Muḥammad Ibn Kathīr, mentioned in the chapter *Meaning and Height of the Spheres, Size of the Fixed Stars*, was a Persian astrologer and astronomer who lived in the 9th century. His work called *Elements* was translated by John of Seville in 1135 and by Gerard of Cremona in about 1175. Printed editions of John of Seville's translation appeared in 1493, 1537 and 1546 under the title *Elementa astronomica*. The influence of this work on the medieval West is undoubted as it spread the knowledge about Ptolemaic astronomy all over Europe. Astrologers like Bonatti and Lilly used Alfraganus' *Elementa astronomica* as a source for their own writing.

Alchindus. Al-Kindī, Abū Yūsuf Yaʿqūb ibn Isḥāq al-Ṣabbāḥ, (also known as Alkindus) who lived between c.801 and 873 CE, was an Arab polymath. He is also known as the "philosopher of the Arabs"; during his lifetime he wrote hundreds of books on astrology, astronomy, mathematics, music, meteorology, and so forth. Mainly known in the West were the translations *De pluviis, imbribus et ventis ac aeris mutatione* (Rains, Storms and Winds, and

---

[1] Pingree, David: "Abū Maʿshar Al-Balkhī, Jaʿfar Ibn Muḥammad." Complete Dictionary of Scientific Biography. 2008. p36f

[2] Ibid, p36

Change in the Air) and *De iudiciis astrorum* (Judgement of the Stars), due to their publication by Peter Liechtenstein at Venice in 1507.

Butzahan. Abu al-Wafa' Buzjani (mainly known as Abu al-Wafa but referred to as Butzahan in the context of *Astronomia Teutsch*) was a Persian mathematician and astronomer. Meyerhof writes about him in his *Biographical Work on Learned Men of the Islam*:

> "The Sage ABU'L WAFA AL-BUZAJANI (93). "He reached the highest place in the geometrical and arithmetical sciences, and his achievement was praiseworthy. Witness of that is his work entitled "The Mansions (of the Moon)" (al-Mandzil); so are his astronomical tables and the rest of his works. He was pure of bosom (heart), disinteresting himself (94) in this world, and content with what he had."... His full name is MUHAMMAD B. MUH. B. YAHYA B. ISMA'IL B. AL-'ABBAS. He was born at Buzajan, a place in East Persia between Herat and Nishapur, in 328/940 and died in 387/997.[3]

Cardanus. Gerolamo Cardano (also known under his Latin name Hieronymus Cardanus) was an Italian Renaissance astrologer and physician who lived between 1501 and 1576. Cardanus' name is mentioned in the title of a short piece (*Explanation of the Things Mentioned Above. D. Hieronymi Cardani / Medici Mediolanem*), following a chapter allegedly written by Ptolemy (*Claudius Ptolemy / Of Rising and Setting / Significance and Influence / of the Changes in the Sky...*). Although Cardanus published an edition of Ptolemy's *Quadripartite*, including a commentary, this only appeared in print in 1555.[4]

Ambrosius Theodosius Macrobius, who is mentioned in the chapter *Of the Movement of Heavens and Planets,* was a Roman Neoplatonist philosopher who lived between 395 and 423 CE. He is the author of a commentary on

---

[3] Meyerhof, Max: *'Ali al-Bayhaqi's Tatimmat Siwan al-Hikma: A Biographical Work on Learned Men of the Islam*, Osiris, Vol. 8 (1948), pp. 122-217

[4] According to Anthony Grafton's *Cardano's Cosmos*, USA 1999, p96

Cicero's *Somnium Scipionis* (Scipio's Dream). This work, being based on the principles of Ptolemy's ideas of the cosmos, was very popular throughout the Middle Ages.

Messahalla. Masha'allah ibn Atharī (740 – 815 CE) was one of the leading astrologers of the late 8th century. He participated in the founding of Baghdad in 762, when a group of astrologers worked on an electional chart to find the best time for the founding of the city. He is mentioned in the chapter *Of the Lord of the Year*. The author is probably referring to Messahalla's *De revolutionibus annorum mundi* (Revolutions of the years of the world). The Arabic original is lost but a Latin translation was published by Bonetus Locatellus at Venice in 1493 and 1519, and by Joachim Heller at Nuremberg in 1549.

Claudius Ptolemy (c.90 AD – c.168 CE) was a mathematician, astrologer, astronomer and geographer. He lived in Egypt under Roman rule and wrote in Greek. His most important works are *Apotelesmatika*, or *Almagest* ("Astrological outcomes" or "effects"), and *Tetrabiblos*, or *Quadripartitum* ("four books") in Latin. *Quadripartitum* was published by Johannes Hervagius at Basle in 1533. Ptolemy is generally classed as the foremost astrologer of the Classical world. Although it is not the place here to discuss the question if his *Tetrabiblos* is the most important source book of astrology, as many astrologers claim, it has to be said that Ptolemy's works had a tremendous influence on the Islamic world and the medieval West. This can be seen by the fact that Ptolemy is referred to throughout the whole of *Astronomia Teutsch*. He is mentioned in the chapters *On the Four Parts of Heaven, The Eighth Heaven, The Seven Climates, Of the Lord of the Year, Of the Rising and Setting, Meaning and height of the Sphere, Rules and Indications to judge Eclipses, Rules and Indications to judge Comets* and *Of Shape and Size of Comets*. I have not been able to identify the work with the title "*Script*" but it is possible that the author refers to a work wrongly attributed to Ptolemy. Ptolemy's "last book of one hundred sayings" is mentioned in the text as well. This is what is generally known as the *Centiloquium*, or "One hundred Sayings", a text attributed to, but certainly not written by Ptolemy.

John of Sacrobosco, also known as John of Hollywood was an English (or possibly Irish or Scottish) astronomer who lived between ca. 1195 and ca. 1256. He is best known for his work *Tractatus de Sphaera*, which was first published about 1230. In his book John of Sacrobosco gives an account of the Ptolemaic universe, making it the successor of Alfraganus' work, mentioned above. At the beginning of the 14th century Konrad von Megenberg translated parts of Sacrobosco's work into German. His work was called *Sphære*, being a compendium of astronomy and physics.

In the original, the *Astronomia* is a loose collection of different texts in no apparent order. To give it a more orderly appearance and to enhance its usability as an astrological textbook, I have rearranged the chapters by grouping them in appropriate parts, labelled: Signs and Images, Planets, Mundane Astrology, Weather, Perpetual Calendar, and Astronomy.

Signs and Images

The first chapter of the first part, "Signs and Images", with the title *Of the Twelve Heavenly Signs*, is an explanation of the nature of the Zodiac, followed by a chapter on the twelve signs and their stars. Here we find that our author decided to present the attributes of the twelve zodiacal signs together with attributes allocated to the constellations of the same name. It is common knowledge amongst astrologers these days that, for the last 2000 years, there were two differing Zodiacs, which, due to the precession of the equinox, overlay each other in an a-synchronous manner. The tropical Zodiac, mainly used in the West, is based on the solstices and equinoxes, whilst the sidereal Zodiac, used in the East, is based upon the ecliptical constellations. In other words, each of the twelve "signs" in the tropical Zodiac consists of a 30° segment, measured from 0° Aries at the Spring Equinox, but each "sign" in the sidereal Zodiac refers to one of the twelve original constellations which have the same names. These are of irregular shape and size. At present, each of the twelve sidereal figures in the sky is overlaid by 80 per cent of the following regular tropical sign. Although there may seem to be confusion about the issue in the original text, we find in another text in this collection, called *The Eighth Heaven* (fully reproduced in the chapter "Astronomy"), that the astrologers of the 15th century were very much aware of the problem:

> "Ptolemy writes in Quadripartito / that the twelve signs have mighty powers from the common stars which are in them / and one has to realise / that the heavenly signs have a different effect in our time / than they had in Ptolemy's time compared to our time which is the year 1410 a.d. / xxv degrees and more / and therefore are now the stars in Aries / which were in Pisces at the time / and the ones that were in Aries are now in Taurus / and so forth through the twelve signs / Whoever wants to know the effects of the Planets in each [sign] / has to observe the common stars / at which place they are located in our time / and has to combine the nature of the stars with the nature of the Planets /"

What the author of this passage means is quite simply that both the tropical as well as the sidereal Zodiac should be taken into account when a thorough interpretation of the relevant stars is undertaken. The difference between the tropical and the sidereal Zodiacs, caused by the precession of the equinox, which increases by 1° in every 72 years, is called *ayanamsa*. Although opinions as to which star should be the starting point of the sidereal Zodiac are manifold, I would recommend using the Lahiri ayanamsa, which seems to be accepted by most Vedic practitioners. The Lahiri ayanamsa for 2000 is 23° 51'. This means that, for example, the tropical span of the constellation of the Bull, in the year 2000 would be between 28° 48' Aries and 25° 30' Taurus, but sidereally it would be between 4° 57' Aries and 1° 39' Taurus (Lahiri).

Constellation	Tropical	Lahiri
The Ram	28♈48 – 25♉30	04♈57 – 01♉39
The Bull	17♉54 – 00♋12	24♈04 – 06♊21
The Twins	00♋00 – 28♋30	06♊09 – 04♋39
The Crab	26♋00 – 20♌18	02♋00 – 26♋27
The Lion	12♌42 – 24♍24	18♋51 – 00♍33
The Virgin	appr 21♍ – 10♏	appr 27♌ – 16♎
The Scales	appr 06♏ – 03♐	appr 12♎ – 09♏
The Scorpion	00♐00 – 00♑00	06♏09 – 06♐09
The Archer	appr 26♐ – 03♒	appr 02♐ – 09♑
The Goat	28♑40 – 28♒40	05♑49 – 05♒49
The Waterman	04♒24 – 28♓27	10♑33 – 04♒36
The Fishes	14♓12 – 05♉18	20♒21 – 11♈27

The following chapters *Pictures of the Heavenly Bodies* and *Of the Fixed Stars and their Qualities* list 36 constellations and their placement. In the following, I provide updated details about the constellations and some of the most important fixed stars mentioned in the footnotes.

Constellation	Fixed Stars	Tropical	Lahiri
Great Bear		14♋36 – 03♎00	20♊45 – 09♍00
Little Bear		appr 23♊ – 19♏	appr 29♉ – 25♌
	Polaris	28♊34	04♊43
Draco		In almost every sign	
	Antares	09♐46	15♏55
	Rastaban	11♐58	18♏07
	Eltanin	27♐58	04♐07
Hercules		23♎36 - 19♑36	01♎45 - 25♐45
	Ras Algethi	16♐09	22♏18
Corona Boralis		3♏40 - 28♏48	09♎49 - 04♏57
	Alphecca	12♏18	18♎27
Ophiucus		appr 01♐ – 13♑	appr 07♏ – 19♐
	Sabik	17♐58	24♏07

A German Stargazer's Book of Astrology

	Rasalhague	22♐27	28♏36	
Boötes		06♎48 – 17♏24	12♏57 23♎33	–
	Arcturus	24♎14	00♎23	
Auriga		13♊00 – 19♋30	19♉09 25♊39	–
	Capella	21♊51	28♉00	
	Menkalinan	29♊55	06♊04	
Cepheus		18♓18 – 07♋18	24♒27 13♊27	–
Cassiopeia		16♈30 – 17♊12	23♓39 23♉21	–
	Caph	05♉07	11♈16	
	Schedir	07♉47	13♈56	
Pegasus		24♒12 – 15♈42	00♒21 21♓45	–
	Alpheratz (Sirrah)	14♈19	20♓28	
Andromeda		02♈00 – 25♉42	08♓09 01♉51	–
	Mirach	00♉24	06♈33	

A German Stargazer's Book of Astrology

Perseus		11♉54 – 20♊00	18♈03 – 26♈09
	Algol	26♉10	02♉19
Triangulum		appr 02♉ – 20♉	appr 08♈ – 26♉
Columba		06♊00 – 09♋00	12♉09 – 15♊09
Cygnus		appr 28♑ – 08♈	appr 04♑ – 14♓
	Albireio	01♒15	07♑24
Lyra		06♑12 – 07♒54	12♐21 – 14♑03
	Vega	15♑19	21♐28
Aquila		appr 17♑ – 05♒	appr 23♐ – 11♑
	Altair	01♒47	07♑56
Cetus		18♓18 – 21♉00	24♒27 – 27♈09
Eridanus		12♓42 – 16♊42	18♒51 – 22♉51
	Archernar	15♓19	21♒28

22

Delphinus		appr 09♒ – 25♒	appr 15♑ – 01♒
Orion		09♊00 – 06♋30	15♉09 – 12♊39
	Bellatrix	20♊57	27♉06
	Betelgeuse	28♊45	04♊54
Canis Major		03♋30 – 02♌00	09♊39 – 08♋09
	Sirius	14♋05	20♊14
Lepus		06♊30 – 03♋42	12♉39 – 09♊51
Argo		02♋36 – 11♏18	08♊45 – 17♌27
Piscis Austrinus		12♒36 – 08♓00	18♑45 – 14♒09
Ara		17♐00 – 04♑30	23♏09 – 10♐39
Centaurus		04♎18 – 01♐24	10♏27 – 07♐33
	Toliman	29♏29	05♏38
Hydra		appr 07♌ – 22♏	appr 13♋ – 28♎

Canis Minor		18♋00 – 08♌30	24♊09 14♌39	-
	Procyon	25♋41	01♋50	
Equuleus		♏29 – 29♏29	29♏29 29♏29	-
Sagitta (Arrow)		appr 18♑ – 14♒	appr 20♑	24♐ -
Vela		21♌00 – 22♎36	27♋00 26♏45	-

Planets

Part two of the translation is concerned with Planets, dignities and aspects. It begins with a description of the seven Planets' properties, followed by a detailed account of physical appearance attributed to the Planet a person is "born under". To establish this Planet, one has to find what is called the *Almuten Figuris*, otherwise known as the most dignified Planet in the chart. To establish the Almuten Figuris, one has to compute and compare the number of essential dignities each Planet has. The Planet with the highest score will be Almuten Figuris. Here is an example to clarify the process:

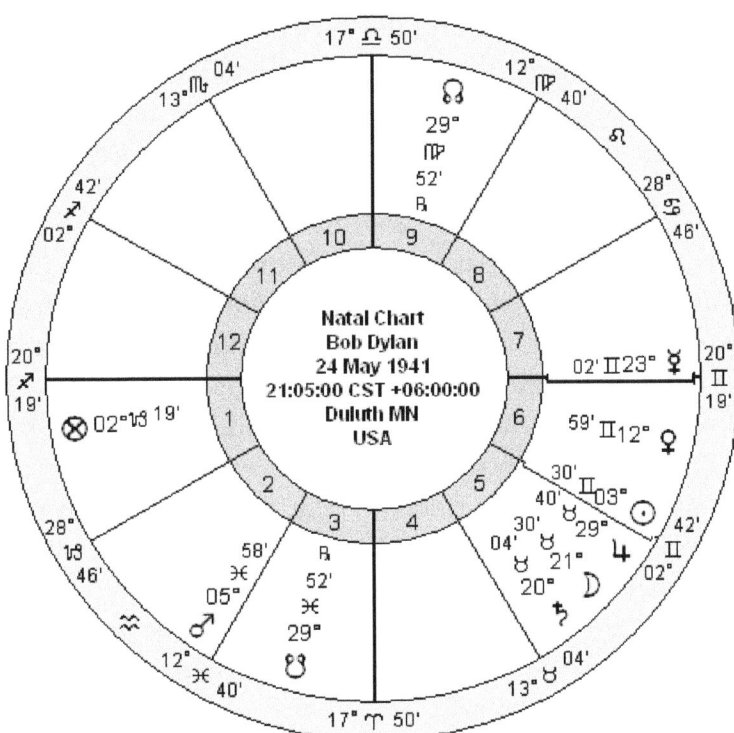

Comparing the essential dignities of the Planets, we find that Mercury is the most essentially dignified Planet in Bob Dylan's birth chart. Looking up the appropriate portion in the translation we find:

> Those born under Mercury / have many colours on them / because they are now white / later black / and have a high noble forehead / and a long nose / and a pretty face / and long and subtle cheeks / and are mediocre / and still a bit plumpish / and like to learn to read and write / and what they begin they will finish soon.

This chapter also includes comments on the effects of Planets when in their planetary hour. The fundamental idea of the day's division into planetary hours is rooted in way of thinking in opposites, whereby our 24 hour day is thought to be split into a dark and a light part. The light part is defined by the length of time between sunrise and sunset and the dark part comprises the hours between sunset and sunrise. For many centuries astrologers have been aware of the fact that the length of day and night is only equal at the equinoxes, whereby its opposite, the longest day and shortest night or vice versa occurs at the solstices.

To establish the planetary hour for any given time, we first have to establish which Planet is ruling the day in question. Monday corresponds to the Moon, Tuesday to Mars, Wednesday to Mercury, Thursday to Jupiter, Friday to Venus, Saturday to Saturn and Sunday to the Sun. To continue with an example, let us assume that we want to find the planetary hours of the Moon for Monday, August 23rd 2010. We already know that Monday is ruled by the Moon; therefore the first planetary hour after sunrise will be a Moon hour (the first hour of the day always being ruled by the ruler of the day). Sunrise is at 05:58UT and sunset is at 20:15UT. Dividing this length of time by 12 we find that the length of each planetary day hour on this particular day is 70 minutes. Therefore the planetary hours ruled by the Moon will be between 05:58UT and 07:08UT and, after all seven planetary hours have passed and another cycle begins, between 14:12UT and 15:22UT.

The following tables show the planetary hours, beginning with the planetary hour of the planetary day (weekday) for the first hour after sunrise:

Hour	Sun	Mon	Tue	Wed	Thu	Fri	Sat
1	☉	☽	♂	☿	♃	♀	♄
2	♀	♄	☉	☽	♂	☿	♃
3	☿	♃	♀	♄	☉	☽	♂
4	☽	♂	☿	♃	♀	♄	☉
5	♄	☉	☽	♂	☿	♃	♀
6	♃	♀	♄	☉	☽	♂	☿
7	♂	☿	♃	♀	♄	☉	☽
8	☉	☽	♂	☿	♃	♀	♄
9	♀	♄	☉	☽	♂	☿	♃
10	☿	♃	♀	♄	☉	☽	♂
11	☽	♂	☿	♃	♀	♄	☉
12	♄	☉	☽	♂	☿	♃	♀

(Planetary Day Hours)

Hour	Sun	Mon	Tue	Wed	Thu	Fri	Sat
1	♃	♀	♄	☉	☽	♂	☿
2	♂	☿	♃	♀	♄	☉	☽
3	☉	☽	♂	☿	♃	♀	♄
4	♀	♄	☉	☽	♂	☿	♃
5	☿	♃	♀	♄	☉	☽	♂
6	☽	♂	☿	♃	♀	♄	☉
7	♄	☉	☽	♂	☿	♃	♀
8	♃	♀	♄	☉	☽	♂	☿
9	♂	☿	♃	♀	♄	☉	☽
10	☉	☽	♂	☿	♃	♀	♄
11	♀	♄	☉	☽	♂	☿	♃
12	☿	♃	♀	♄	☉	☽	♂

(Planetary Night Hours)

The following four chapters of the translation are concerned with the dignities and debilities of the Planets. Here is a table summarising the point system necessary in determining the essential dignity or debility of a Planet. Although not explicitly mentioned in the translation, I have added the scoring system for essential debilities.

Essential Dignity	Score	Essential Debility	Score
Rulership	+5	Peregrine	-5
Exaltation	+4	Detriment	-5
Triplicity	+3	Fall	-5
Term	+2		
Face	+1		

The table below shows the *Essential Dignities and Debilities of the Planets, according to Ptolemy.*

A Table of the Essential Dignities of the PLANETS according to Ptolemy																
Sign	Houses of the Planets		Exalt-ation	Triplicity of Planets		The Terms of the Planets					The Faces of the Planets			Detri ment	Fall
				D	N										
♈	♂	D	☉ 19	☉	♃	♃ 6	♀ 14	☿ 21	♂ 26	♄ 30	♂ 10	☉ 20	♀ 30	♀	♄
♉	♀	N	☽ 3	♀	☽	♀ 8	☿ 15	♃ 22	♄ 26	♂ 30	☿ 10	☽ 20	♄ 30	♂	
♊	☿	D	☊ 3	♄	☿	☿ 7	♃ 13	♀ 21	♄ 25	♂ 30	♃ 10	♂ 20	☉ 30	♃	
♋	☽	D/N	♃ 15	♂	♂	♂ 6	♃ 13	☿ 20	♀ 27	♄ 30	♀ 10	☿ 20	☽ 30	♄	♂
♌	☉	D/N		☉	♃	♄ 6	☿ 13	♀ 19	♃ 25	♂ 30	♄ 10	♃ 20	♂ 30	♄	
♍	☿	N	☿ 15	♀	☽	☿ 7	♀ 13	♃ 18	♄ 24	♂ 30	☉ 10	♀ 20	☿ 30	♃	♀
♎	♀	D	♄ 21	♄	☿	♄ 6	♀ 11	♃ 19	☿ 24	♂ 30	☽ 10	♄ 20	♃ 30	♂	☉
♏	♂	N		♂	♂	♂ 6	♃ 14	♀ 21	☿ 27	♄ 30	♂ 10	☉ 20	♀ 30	♀	☽
♐	♃	D	☋ 3	☉	♃	♃ 8	♀ 14	☿ 19	♄ 25	♂ 30	☿ 10	☽ 20	♄ 30	☿	
♑	♄	N	♂ 28	♀	☽	♀ 6	☿ 12	♃ 19	♂ 25	♄ 30	♃ 10	♂ 20	☉ 30	☽	♃
♒	♄	D		♄	☿	♄ 6	☿ 12	♀ 20	♃ 25	♂ 30	♀ 10	☿ 20	☽ 30	☉	
♓	♃	N	♀ 27	♂	♂	♀ 8	♃ 14	☿ 20	♂ 26	♄ 30	♄ 10	♃ 20	♂ 30	☿	☿

This table provides all the information needed to calculate the essential dignity or debility for each Planet in a chart.

To come back to our example chart, we can now have another look at Bob Dylan's Mercury, who is in 23♊02. Using the table of essential dignities, we find that Mercury in this position is in his domicile and triplicity. According to the suggested point system, this would allocate eight points to Mercury. Comparing this to the other Planets, we find that the Moon in 21♉30, scores seven points (exaltation +4, triplicity +3), the Sun in 03♊30, scores two points (term +2), and so forth, making Mercury Almuten Figuris, the strongest Planet in the chart.

The tables for the Egyptian Terms, mentioned but not included in the text, can be found in Appendix A.

Mundane Astrology

Part three is concerned with mundane astrology, including chapters on the Revolution of the Year, the Lord of the Year, conjunctions, eclipses and comets. The Revolution of the Year was used as an important indicator for mundane astrologers, providing them with a powerful tool to predict the events of the year ahead. To demonstrate this technique, the following is a practical example, showing the Aries ingress chart, or Revolution of the Year 2010, cast for London.

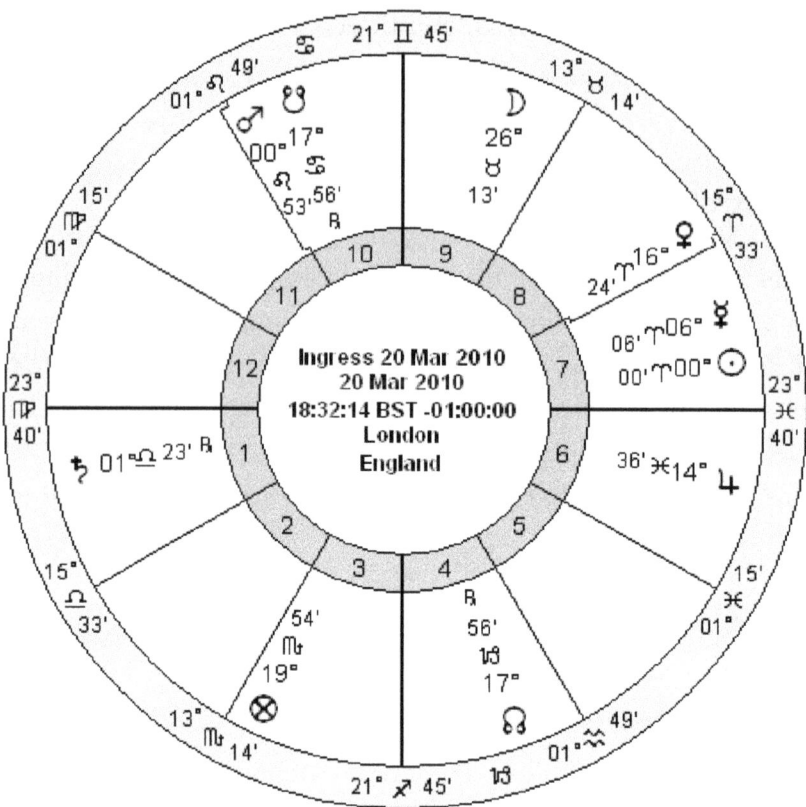

Applying the rules according to the text, we can see that Saturn is in the first house. Therefore he has to be Lord of the Year 2010. The sign on the Ascendant, Virgo, is a mutable sign and therefore Saturn will only be Lord of the Year until the Sun has moved on to 00° Libra, when a new ingress chart will have to be cast. The chapter called *Significance of Lords and Houses* provides detailed information about the effects the different Lords of the Year would have on the country the ingress chart is cast for.

The following chapter *Of Dignity and Elevation of one Planet Above the Other* does not   provide the reader with instructions for calculating a Planet's "elevation".

The term elevation was used by the astrologer Ibn Ezra, who claimed in his book *The Beginning of Wisdom*, that a Planet would be strengthened in "its place of elevation"[5]. This seems to refer to what is called the auge but does not provide any information on how to distinguish which Planet would be elevated over another.[6] The fact that lunar nodes and comets are also included in the chapter does not make the situation any clearer. Judging from the last paragraph in this chapter, it seems though that elevation was seen to be as important as conjunctions and aspects between the Planets.

Weather

The following part draws together the different chapters of the translation, dealing with astrological weather prognostication. The chapter on the *Twelve Centers of the Moon* is of particular interest here. We do not know the author of this particular text but it seems that it differs considerably from other known versions. Guido Bonatti, the famous 13th century astrologer, wrote about the centers of the Moon in his *Book of Astronomy*. Dr. Ben Dykes, who published a translation of Bonatti's work in 2007[7], states that Bonatti drew his information about the centers of the Moon from the Arab astrologer Jafar Indus. According to Dr Dykes, the information in Jafar is distorted or incomplete, only providing information about eight of the twelve centers[8]. The text included here seems to provide more detailed information, making it possible to find the exact positions of each of the twelve centers. The following table illustrates this.

---

[5] Ibn Ezra: *The Beginning of Wisdom*, trans. Meira B. Epstein, Arhat Publications, 1998, p105.

[6] For more information about the term auge, see appendix B.

[7] Bonatti, Guido: *Book of Astronomy*, trans. Dr Ben Dykes, Cazimi Press, Minnesota 2007, vol 2, p1417ff.

[8] ibid, p 1426, fn 57.

Centre	1	2	3	4	5	6	7	8	9	10	11	12
Angle	00°	12°	30°	40°	45°	48°	180°	192°	210°	220°	225°	228°

Of the opening of the Planetary Portals comprises the different movements of the Planets and luminaries which are claimed to open "Planetary Portals". It seems that these "portals" were considered to cause changes in the atmosphere and, once activated or "opened", would bring down a form of bad weather or heavy rain onto the Earth. The text does not include any information about the kind of weather that would be unleashed by each individual portal. Although our author provides a different explanation of the portals, we can gain some additional information from the Arab astrologer Al Biruni's *Book of Instructions*[9]. He explains that "the conjunction of Sun or Moon with Saturn indicates quiet rain, fine drizzle or snowstorms, that of Venus and Mars torrential rain, hail, thunder and lightning, and that of Mercury and Jupiter the opening of the doors of the winds". In a footnote we read: "if you see the Moon separate from Venus and apply itself to Mars or v. v., this is also opening of the doors:" Haly, p. 396.

Perpetual Calendar

The following is an alphabetical tabulation of the fixed stars and constellations mentioned in the chapter *Of the Changes in the Sky throughout the Year*.

---

[9] Al Biruni: *The Book of Instructions in the Elements of the Art of Astrology,* [Ghazana, 1029 A.D. tr. Ramesy Wright, 1934] Astrology Classics, 2006, p88.

A German Stargazer's Book of Astrology

Andromeda:
is rising on August 28th
Aquarius:
is appearing on January 20th
is completely visible on January 21st
is appearing on February 9th
begins to rise on February 24th
Aquila:
is setting on January 1st and January 5th
is setting in the evening of January 6th
is rising on May 23rd and June 2nd and 5th
is setting in the mornings of July 30th and August 1st
is setting on July 23rd, 26th and August 2nd
is setting completely in the evening of October 31st
is rising on December 7th
is rising in the evening of December 22nd
Argo:

	becomes visible in the evening of March 13th
	is descending on September 21st
Aries:	
	is visible at times on March 21st
	becomes visible in the morning of March 25th
	its centre is setting with Scorpio on October 6th
Auriga:	
	is setting on October 3rd
Betelgeuse: [28♊45, Sun transits these longitudes between June 18th and June 22nd]	
	is elevated on June 14th
	is appearing on June 17th
Cancer:	
	is setting on January 3rd
	its centre is setting on January 20th
	is setting on January 22nd
	is rising backwards on March 22nd
	is rising on May 15th

	its centre is rising on July 5th
	as a whole is rising together with Leo on July 23rd
	is descending on July 24th
Canis Major:	
	is rising in the morning of January 4th
	is setting in the evening of April 30th
	is hiding on May 1st
	becomes visible on June 27th
	is rising in the morning of June 29th
	becomes visible on July 25th
	is setting on November 27th
	is beginning to hide on November 28th
	is setting in the morning of November 29th
	is setting on December 2nd
	is rising in the morning of December 9th
Canis Minor:	
	is rising on July 15th and July 20th
	is rising in the morning of July 18th

Capella: [21♊51, the Sun transits these longitudes between June 10th and June 12th]

> is becoming visible when the Vergilie are setting in the evening of September 29th

> becomes visible on September 6th

> is rising on September 14th

> is setting on December 14th

> is rising on December 19th

> is visible in the morning of December 23rd

Capricorn:

> is rising on January 8th

Cassiopeia:

> is beginning to hide on October 30th

Centaurus:

> becomes visible on May 3rd

> is rising on September 23rd

> is setting in the morning of October 25th

Cepheus:

> is rising on July 8th

Cetus:

    is not hiding anymore on September 1st

Corona:

    is setting on January 1st

    is hiding in the mornings of March 7th and July 7th

    is setting on August 5th

    becomes visible on October 5th

    is rising together with the Hedis on October 8th

    is rising in the morning of October 11th

    becomes visible on October 13th

Crateris:

    is rising on February 14th

    is appearing on September 18th

Cygnus:

    is visible on March 9th

    is beginning to decline on March 10th

Delphinius:

    is rising in the morning of January 4th

is setting in the morning of January 18th
is beginning to set on January 29th
is setting in the evening of February 4th
is beginning to appear on June 8th
becomes visible on June 13th
is setting in the morning of August 13th
is hiding on August 16th
is rising on August 23rd

Gemini:

is rising on May 23rd
is beginning to set on July 25th

Hedi:

are rising on April 29th and September 25th
are rising together with the Sun on September 26th
are rising on October 4th
are visible on October 9th

Hyades:

are becoming visible on April 6th

	are hiding on April 12th
	are setting on April 15th, 16th and 17th
	are setting completely on April 19th
	are setting on April 21st
	are setting same time as the Sun on May 2nd
	are setting on May 10th and May 13th
	are rising on May 20th
	are beginning to rise on May 24th
	become visible on June 1st
	are setting on October 27th
	are setting together with Lepus in the morning of November 21th
Leo:	
	is hiding on January 14th
	is setting in the morning of January 18th
	its centre is setting with Lyra on February 3rd
	is setting on February 20th
	is rising together with the Sun and with Canis Major on July 24th
	is rising on July 26th

	its centre is appearing on August 4th
	its centre is rising on August 5th
	is rising on August 8th
Libra:	
	is visible in the morning of March 18th
	is beginning to rise on October 10th
Little Crabs:	
	are rising on April 13th
	are rising on April 25th
Lyra:	
	is rising on January 5th
	is beginning to set on January 17th
	is setting on January 22nd and January 26th
	is setting in the evenings of January 27th and January 30th
	is beginning to set on February 1st and February 3rd
	is setting on February 7th
	appears on April 23rd
	is visible on April 24th

is rising in the morning of May 5th
is rising on May 10th
is rising in the mornings of May 14th and May 28th
is completely visible on August 6th
is setting in the morning of August 11th
is setting on August 15th
is setting in the morning of August 17th
is rising on October 31st
is rising in the morning of November 3rd
appears at the time the Sun rises on November 5th
is rising in the morning of November 15th

Malus:

is setting in the evening of February 18th
is hidden on February 19th
is setting in the evening of February 27th
is visible in the next two days from August 4th
is hiding on September 3rd

Ophiuchus:

	is rising in the morning of June 20th
Orion:	
	its belt becomes visible on February 5th
	is rising in the morning on June 18th
	is rising on June 22nd and June 26th
	its belt is appearing on June 29th
	is rising on July 4th
	is completely visible on July 9th
	is rising completely in the morning on July 12th
	is rising on July 16th
	can be seen completely on July 19th
	its centre is hiding on August 8th
	girdle's centre is rising on August 8th
	is visible on October 16th
	is setting completely on October 28th
	is setting completely in the evening of October 31st
	is hiding on November 7th
	is setting in the morning of November 13th

	is rising together with Lyra on November 18th
	is setting on November 30th
	is setting in the morning of December 1st
Pegasus:	
	is setting in the morning of March 7th
	is setting on March 8th
	is setting in the morning of March 10th
	is setting on March 15th
	is setting in the mornings of March 20th and March 24th
	is rising on September 5th and September 13th
Pisces:	
	its back begins to disappear in the morning of March 9th
	ceases to rise any further from March 12th
	its back becomes visible on March 25th
	towards the south on September 1st
	is rising on September 17th
	is setting on September 20th and September 22nd

Pleiades: [29♉25, the Sun transits these longitudes between May 19th and May

20th]	
	are beginning to rise on April 1st
	are setting in the evening of April 3rd
	are setting on April 7th and April 8th
	are rising in the morning of May 7th
	appear on May 11th
	are rising on May 12th and May 30th
Procyon: [25♋41, the Sun transits these longitudes between July 15th and July 19th]	
	is setting on May 17th
Sagittarius:	
	is setting on February 13th, May 22nd and December 4th
Scorpio:	
	is setting on March 28th and April 1st
	begins to rise on May 4th
	its middle is setting on May 6th
	is setting on May 14th and October 23rd
	half of its tail is setting on October 26th

is becoming visible on November 12th
is setting in the morning of November 14th
its centre is becoming visible on December 6th
is completely visible on December 8th
the whole of it is rising on December 13th

Taurus:

its head is setting completely on April 26th
its head becomes visible on May 10th
is setting on May 26th
its tail is setting on October 22nd
its horn is setting together with the Sun on November 19th
its horns are setting on November 23rd

Ursa Major:

appears on February 11th
is beginning to disappear on February 21st
becomes visible on February 25th
is rising in the morning of February 26th
is setting in the morning of March 2nd

is rising when the Sun is at its zenith on March 3rd
is still rising on March 4th
is rising on March 10th
is setting on May 21st
is setting in the morning of June 7th
is setting on June 8th
is setting in the morning of June 30th
is hiding on September 3rd
is appearing on September 7th
is rising on September 11th
its centre is visible in the morning of September 18th
is hiding on October 29th and November 1st
is setting in the morning of November 6th

Vergilie:

are rising on September 13th
are visible in the morning and evening of September 26th
can be seen in the morning of September 28th
are becoming visible as they rise on October 1st and October 2nd

	are visible on October 9th
	are rising on October 12th
	are setting on October 20th and October 24th
	are setting completely on October 28th and November 1st
	are hiding on November 7th and November 11th
	are setting in the morning of November 13th
Vindemitor: [09♎56, Sun transits these longitudes between Oct. 1st and Oct. 5th]	
	becomes visible on March 2nd
	is setting on March 10th
	becomes visible on August 24th
	is hiding on September 3rd
Virgo:	
	is setting near Gemini on February 17th
	begins to set on February 18th
	is rising on August 19th
	is rising completely on August 20th and August 21st
	is beginning to appear on August 25th

is rising on August 27th
its centre is rising on September 8th
is not rising any more on September 26th

Astronomy

The last chapter in the translation is devoted to astronomical texts. For a basic graphic, introductory text and additional tables, explaining the basic principles of 16th century astronomy, see appendix B.

Notes on translation, spelling and grammar

Spelling and capitalisation in the original text often do not follow any modern grammatical rules. I have corrected obvious spelling or printing errors but where I have done so the original term is to be found in the footnote if the meaning has been altered. Capitalisation has been gently corrected in the body of the translation where it seemed necessary to improve our understanding of the text's meaning. Words which have fallen out of use are explained in the footnotes. Wherever original German words are quoted in footnotes, the original spelling and capitalisation has been preserved. Additional words added for ease of understanding are marked thus: [word]; words whose meanings have been lost are given in the original German and are marked thus: [wort?]. The word "Planet" is spelled with a capital "P" throughout the text as a reminder that the astrological Planets include the Moon and the Sun although they would not generally be classed as planets in the astronomical sense.

It has to be noted that in modern day High German the Sun is always female and the Moon is always male. Although this may be true in a grammatical sense, in astrological lore these roles are reversed. This contradiction between grammar and the inherent natures of the Sun and Moon has led to some confusing sentences as the examples below show:

Amongst the planets the Sun is actually called father of the day ... and the light the Sun has / she takes from above from God (p2)

Below him God placed the Moon with his sphere / and she is the herald and identifier of all bodies / cold and moist / like the sea and the waters / and the menstruation of women. (p3)

What has to be taken into consideration is the fact that up to the beginning of the 17th century the genders attributed to the Sun and the Moon have been more or less ambivalent in the German language. The brothers Grimm write in their important *German Wörterbuch*, that up to the time of Middle Low German, which was spoken between 1300 and 1600 CE, it was common to refer to the Moon as being either male or female. Similarly the words for our modern day "Sun" used to be *sunna* (feminine) or, in rarer cases, *sunno* (masculine).

Abbreviations used in footnotes:

FSC: Robson, Vivian: *The Fixed Stars & Constellations in Astrology*, Astrology Classics, Abingdon, 2005.

SH: Cornelius, Geoffrey: *The Starlore Handbook,* Duncan Baird, London, 2000

A German Stargazer's Book of Astrology
(Astronomia Teutsch Astronomei 1545)

Preamble
All the works of our merciful God and Father / kind reader / are truly miraculous / and for the benefit of men / that they would recognise / fear / trust and revere / and constantly praise / commend and thank / the Creator / in his power and mercy through those / created. But amongst all carnal creatures the power and wisdom of God seems to be closest [to men] / as David bears witness. The heavens are telling the praise of God / and the firmament proclaims the work of his hands. What is more miraculous to human reason / than the perpetual movement of the firmament / [its] circular motion / taking all the stars with it / differentiating time / day / month and year / warmth / cold / moisture and dryness / working through the order of the Creator. There is no star in the sky / that would not fulfil its work that has been ordered by God / to praise him with all its power. But such things / how and when they would happen / to partially explore / and to gain some basic understanding / the glorious art [of] astrology[10] / which is teaching the motion of the heavens and stars and their influence / is not just of small use. Therein scholars of many nations have most diligently / published / and have worked upon / and some of our forebears have tried to translate this astrology into German / but they were not of the opinion (as some of the ignorant suspect) that the star in itself should be seen as / or itself feared / as if something out of itself would have an effect or influence on the bodies on earth / No / because God has not tied his power onto the stars / but he himself is working through them / as he pleases / for the comfort and the benefit of the faithful / but for the

---

[10] *Astronomia, astronomîe,* Middle High German for *Sterndeutung,* "star gazing".

punishment of the wicked and the ones violating his word / etc. God rather revealed and gave this art to human beings / that through recognition and view of the heavenly creatures / God himself / the just master of the work / and Christ the Lord / through whom everything has been created would be sought / found / recognised / feared / worshipped / vowed / etc. And although a few books / about this astrology / have gone to print in German before / nearly none has (in my opinion) gone ever as far as this one in German and explained / than this one that my very dear friend / Hans Orth von Bacharach / a lover of astrology / in a very old handwritten book / for the good of all Germans / has sent to me / wherein you will [find] much / of comets / and other [things] which have not been seen in print in German ever before / which you / dear reader / can make use of by reading / God's mighty power / unspeakable wisdom and eternal benevolence / in his heavenly works / perceive with praise and gratitude / with fear and betterment of your life / want to view and make use of / this shall be bestowed to you through Jesus Christ our saviour / to whose grace you are commanded now.

Of the Nine Spheres of Heaven

Above the firmament is the ninth heaven or sphere / in the same heaven are God and God's angels / and all souls who are just / This ninth heaven is called Empirium / that is the fiery heaven / because it is a secret place of mighty power / and it is hidden[11] from the people on earth / [it is] the throne upon which deity is sitting / a heaven of the uppermost trinity called Thronus / or the chair of the most high / he is a true Emperor / and a King of all kings / and a Master of all rulers / and in this ninth heaven there is no star and no planet / because this heaven is adorned with the highest Light of the brightness of God / and it is adorned in a way / that nobody may talk or write about it.

---

[11] *verholen*

The eighth sphere is called the firmament of heaven / and therein are all the stars according to their order / and the stars are equal to the twelve signs of heaven / and it is said about these same stars that they are in the order of the xxxvi pictures of heaven / which is called firmament / and this is turned around more mightily than all the other wheels of movement / and out of this fast rotation comes such mighty heat / that the stars and the air have too much heat in them caused by the heat and warmth / and therefore has God / who is the highest artificer above it / put another heaven / which is called crystal heaven / and this heaven has the shape and form of pure water / and frozen ice / stronger than a crystal / and the cold of this crystal heaven withstands the warmth of the fiery heat / [and] a wheel is turning there / and God has set the firmament amidst the waters / and separates the waters from the waters / and it should not be understood that the crystal heaven is a heaven in itself / otherwise there would be ten spheres / but there are only nine.

Below this sphere lies the heaven of Saturn / most cold and clear / equal to water or snow / or the nature of quicksilver / and the ice in this sphere comes from the force of its body / because Saturn is the coldest and driest / so that the heat of the uppermost sphere might not fall down / because it would bring harm / that the whole of the earth would burn / and this is why Saturn is put in the heaven / because he is the origin of coldness.

Therefore God has ordered the heaven or sphere of Mars / who is hot and dry / so that the earth would not be too cold / his influence is called Arsura / which is heat / which is most dry / and through his warmth God has placed Mars the planet.

But God recognised that there would be too much of this planet in the world / so God placed in between the planets Saturn and Mars / Jupiter and his sphere / he is one who is a mediator[12] and intermediary between Saturn and Mars / and therefore Jupiter is a moderate planet / mild and good / is of

---

[12] *zunemer*

use to all people / and is always standing strong in the quarrel of the two evils.

Below Mars God has set the Sun / virtuous and in her[13] sphere / amongst the planets the Sun is actually called father[14] of the day / and prince of the planets / and enlightens up there as well as down here / and the light the Sun has / she takes from above from God / and then the Moon takes it from the Sun.

Below the Sun God placed Venus in his sphere.

Below Venus God placed Mercury with his sphere.

Below him God placed the Moon with his sphere / and she is the herald and identifier of all bodies / cold and moist / like the sea and the waters / and the menstruation of women.

Below the Moon there is no star or planet / only the whole width of the four elements in their order.

On top He put fire / and thereafter air / thereafter water / earth in fourth place / and in the middle of the Earth there is Hell / and therein are the cursed spirits for eternity / and the damned souls coming therein.

---

[13] Note that in German the Sun is female.

[14] For an explanation of the discrepancy between the Sun's gender and the traditional masculine interpretation see my introduction.

Part One

SIGNS and IMAGES

Of the Nine Spheres of Heaven

Of the Twelve Heavenly Signs / and why they are named thus

The firmament of heaven is a sphere or circle / wherein the stars are. Below this circle there is another circle / called zodiacus / in this zodiac there are the twelve heavenly signs / these are named after some animals / as they are on earth or in the water / But this is not the reason why they are shaped like a ram or bull / [it is] because they are named after the nature and characteristics of these twelve animals / because the characteristics and effects of the signs / when the Sun or Moon is in them / are as found in these animals.

The first sign is called Aries, a ram / because a ram is very hairy[15] / and is naturally drawn towards unchastity / and he likes to shout / As well when the Sun is in Aries / the earth is sprouting / the roots / the trees / and the leaves are becoming green / the fountains and the waters are waking up / and people are ready to do unchaste things / because at this time the humidity of the blood is growing in most animals.

The other sign is called Taurus an ox / Because like an ox / who does not get tired / and drinking little or nothing during work / he is steady and strong / Also when the Sun is in Taurus / it is full of work / and stays well and strong / and is steadfast in good things / like the people who work in garden / field / acre and vines / but who often do not enjoy much of their fruit and wine.

---

15 *harecht*

The third sign is called Gemini twins / this sign is like two humans / who are naked / and are looking at each other all the time / and when the Sun is standing in this sign / the animals are not working or carrying much / but they are happy / and are feeding well on the growing fruits of the earth.

The fourth sign is called Cancer a crab / Because like a crab walking forwards / and then walking backwards / It is the same when the Sun comes in this sign / she begins to move backwards / after she was moving forwards up to this point / and in the same way the earth grows with it.

The fifth sign is called Leo a lion / because the lion is bigger and stronger in his front part / and he is very hairy and keen / It is the same at the time when the Sun is in the lion / because from the beginning to the end of this sign / there is much heat and warmth / which is strong by day and night.

The sixth sign is called Virgo virgin / because like the maid is modest naturally / and of an emotional disposition[16] and weak strength / and is longing to get a husband easily / and is hesitant on the surface [to be] without dishonour. The same applies when the Sun is in the sign / it is a happy time / and there is much fruit on the field / corn in the barn / cheese / wool / honey and wax / but this time will soon be changing into something bad / and does not last long.

The seventh sign is called Libra the scales / because it is equally burdened like the scales / and administers justice / showing the truth / the Sun is doing the same / when she is in Libra / day and night are of equal length / and all people request what is theirs / and governs / it is a sign for the midpoint of time / because two ages of the year have passed / spring and summer / and two more are about to come / autumn and winter.

---

[16] *beweglichen Herzens*, lit. of a moving heart.

The eighth sign is called Scorpio a scorpion[17] / because Scorpio is an evil animal / and of terrifying shape / and has a deceitful face / and first it flatters / and afterwards it stings / and likes to be in the ground and in hidden places / equally when the Sun is in Scorpio / the time will be wrong / now it is summer then it is winter / with winds / rime / cold / and rain / and the days are shortening / and it is [a] bad fearful time.

The ninth sign is called Sagittarius an archer / because it holds its bow like an archer / ready to shoot / equally when the Sun is in Sagittarius / she lets harmful blows into the world / as cold / wind / rain / snow / ice / and rime / which causes need in the world / and saddens people.

The tenth sign is called Capricornus an ibex / this is an animal with horns and a beard / of cold and dry nature / shorthaired / simple / and gives milk / equally when the Sun is in Capricorn / it is not colder in any other month / this time is cold and dry in nature / the soil is unable to bear anything / and the water as well / and the crop [literally "plants"] of people is little and feeble[18] / and [they are] working a little bit / when it is warm.

The eleventh sign is called Aquarius a water bearer / because like the water bearer it brings water in a bucket and spreads it / equally when the Sun is in Aquarius / this time brings snow and rain / and people wear hats etc.

The twelfth sign is called Pisces fishes / because fishes are always mobile and are living in water / equally when the Sun is in Pisces / it will be very moist at this time / darkness and rain / and the ground is watery / and people will move lazily.

---

[17] *tarant*, Middle High German word for "scorpion" or "spider", also used as a name for the zodiac sign Scorpio.

[18] The use of the word *torecht* (from Middle High German *tôrëhtic*) in this context is questionable as the original meaning of it has to be translated as "foolish" or "stupid".

The characteristics mentioned above may generally be found in people born under these signs / if a person will be conceived or born in these signs / their complexion will be according to the nature of these animals now drawn to this one and later to that one. So that the reader will be able to gain knowledge about the twelve signs and the xxxvi. images / including their properties / and will be able to judge the ways and customs of the people / we want to explain them one after the other.

Of the Twelve Signs their Stars and Effects

Aries

Aries is the diurnal house of the planet Mars / and has xx. stars / their disposition and distribution is as follows / In each horn is one [and] on the forehead one / on the nose three / on the neck two / on the back four / on the belly three / at the end of each of the four legs one / on the tail one. But who will be conceived or born under this sign / he is naturally rich and full of riches / mundane goods or mental [ones] / and not much mundane / he is keen and cheeky in his deeds / he is strong / and a bit verbose[19] / he is belligerent in many ways / and is still wise in his work and ingenious in his life / and will be harmed a lot because of being beaten / as an animal of this kind would be / and will be very unchaste at times / and likes to visit many kingdoms and many foreign lands / he will be one who does a lot and spends a lot / and a liar and a cheat / and a whoremonger and murderer / and is doing many good things at another time / he moves easily / and is very mobile / and is very similar to this animal in nearly all ways / in natures and virtues / this shall be understood according to the virtues of the parts of the degree of the ascendant.

Aries has the face of a goat / and has small stars in the eyes and intestines / and causes illnesses in the eyes and ears of people / When the Moon is in Aries the rising[20] sign / and a person is born / he is hot and a choleric /

---

[19] *weitschweiffig*

[20] Reading "rising" for *Oriental*.

[kubisch?][21] / and it will be good if he will begin to journey towards the orient / and in this part it is beneficial to run or travel because of the treasures of a merchant / and who will begin his path in this part / his journey will be pleasant and fulfilled / it will be well achieved / what you can achieve with fire.

It is beneficial to let [blood] at the arms / and to have a bath / and for work that needs to be finished and not prolonged / It is bad to wash the head / medicines or cupping with cupping glasses[22] / clipping / or letting blood from the nose / and to marry housewives / or to start building a castle where you are ruling / and to leave prison / And as the ram is an animal that is regurgitating / one should not take any medicines / because if it is taken / it will repeat on one. The same goes for all regurgitating signs / being Aries / Taurus / and Capricorn / if the sign is rising in the east[23] / it will be a warm time.

Taurus

Taurus is Venus' nocturnal house / and has xviii. stars / and they are in the head / they are called Hyades in Greek / but Sucule in Latin / under these the vapours are lifting up in the air / where they will be overcome / where they will be transformed into clouds / and afterwards into rain. There are two stars on the forehead of Taurus called Hyades / they rise mightily at the time of autumn / There are [some] at the backmost part of Taurus where the arse or tail is / called Pleiades in Greek / Vergilie in Latin / and these seven stars are called the hen and the chicks by the people / and they rise at the time of spring / and appear all night / when they set it will be the beginning of winter and the overcoming of time / when they begin to shine

---

[21] So far I have not been able to find this word in any dictionary or gain any knowledge of its meaning.

[22] *ventusen*

[23] *orient*

at the time of spring / the rope[24] will be cut / and sailors [will be] at sea / after they shine clear after an obscure or dark time / this will be recognised through the wind or direction / if it is a clear and quiet time / they proclaim it on sea and land / and there again if they appear obscured or dark or foggy. Their order is like this / in each horn one / on the forehead two / on the nose one / on each knee one / on the nail of the right foot two / on each shoulder one / at the throat one / at the back are three / and the backmost is much larger than the others / on the chest one / on the belly one / at the end of the tail one star.

Who will be conceived or born under Taurus / will be lucky / like a bull and will live to work all the time / in body and in mind / he always works hard and will become rich late in life / This one will be more chaste then unchaste / and unfortunate / and receives evil / but more from those who try to do him good / and receives more blessings from strangers than from the locals for his benefit.

Taurus has neck and throat / and what comes to him in days of sickness and afflictions / which is a residue[25] from the nose / and a hunch[26] of the back or pain in the eyes / which will take a long time to heal. When the Moon is in Taurus / which is a fixed sign and of the south[27] / cold and dry / and melancholy / and fertile / and feminine / and then it is good to take wives / and doing the garden and wines and planting of trees / because they like to grow and will last / and it is good to build castles and lasting buildings / and to lead women to church / beginning of all defences / and what you

---

[24] The text uses the word *marn*, deriving from Middle High German *merren*, "to tether", "lash" or "rack up".

[25] The German word used here is *Trusen*. According to Grimm's *Deutsches Wörterbuch*, *Trusen* are defined as "dregs" or "residue"; the word fell out of use in the 17th century.

[26] *hufer*, from *hüfern*, "to bend".

[27] *mittäglich*

like to accomplish soon / the time will be cold and dry / the clouds will be hanging low / returning[28] through air or water / and there are generally mists.

Gemini

Gemini is Mercury's diurnal house / and has xix. stars / the sign of two figures and each is of human form and they seem to be more naked than clothed / and standing close to each other like two people who would like to go with each other / and one has a stick in the right hand / as if it would hit the other / cheeky / impudent / and the other has a lyre in the left hand / the first figure has ix. stars / their order is as follows on the head it has i. that is very clear / on each shoulder i. very clear / and i. large star on the elbow / on the right hand i. on each knee i. on each foot i. the other sign has x. stars their distribution is shown as well / on the head it has i. large one which is clear / and two large ones on the breasts. i. large clear star on the left elbow / and has ii. in the left hand / and one on the left knee / and on each foot one but at the left foot is standing one called Propiis.[29]

Who will be conceived or born under this sign / he will be of good understanding / and likes to work / and will be very wise / has a good memory / rich in property and virtues / He is reputable and prudish and fearful / and is easily converted to evil or to good / and has much luck / and many good things will come his way / and disappear again easily / and his heart is always open for many things / and under this sign nobody should confirm anything / or marry a woman / neither lead a housewife into his house / and if it happens that two join on this day / they will never love each other / and never live well with love.

---

[28] *Wider lauffen*, Middle High German *widerloufe*, to return to.

[29] *Propus*, from the Greek, meaning "forward foot"; strangely in *FSC*, Robson places it "between the shoulders of the twins" (p193), stating its influence would be "of the nature of Mercury and Venus. It gives strength, eminence and success" (ibid).

Gemini has the armpits and the arms and the hands / and the shoulders / And if the Moon is in Gemini / in the double setting sign / which is warm moist and airy / joyful / cheeky and masculine / It is good to make friends / good to start an argument / it is evil to medicate the arms / or to cut the nails on the hands / or let blood on the arms / and the barber has to tap[30] twice / and even then the blood will hardly come out / and after a while the arm will be lame / and sometimes it dies. The time is warm and moist / and it is a good time / but it is not a good time to start travelling / because the journey will split and therefore has to be begun twice / what is begun / But it is beneficial to take medicine / but never in the aforementioned places over which the sign has power / like the arms / armpits and hands.

Cancer

Cancer is the diurnal and nocturnal house of the Moon / and is the fourth sign in the heavens / and has xviii. stars / and their distribution is shown as follows / on the fourth horn are ii. on the other horn are ii. as well but the first two are larger and clearer / the other ii. are never shining / because they are a bit dark / its name is Honi and there is a star with the crab / like a crab[31] / and the peasants call it that / and in his mouth he has a large clear star / and on the right side / on each leg i. and they are a bit darker and not clear / and therefore they are called the four dark stars / it is as well true that the [stars] in the first two legs on the left side are a bit clearer than the others / and on his back he has two / and at the end of the tail he has iii. / some of the masters say there are iii. some [say] ii. [note in right margin:] Biginus does not count any on the tail.

Who will be born or conceived under this sign will be lucky and unlucky / like the crab in all things / and will always be fearful / ill / quiet and not

---

[30] The word *schlagen* used in the original means "to beat" in German, which is slightly unclear in this context. This appears to be part of the bloodletting process, e.g. finding a vein through tapping the area.

[31] *krypff*

shouting / and has much luck with possessions / which will not stay with him for long / his hope grows / and fails to grow / and [he] suffers much because of contempt through other people's business / and is doing more for strangers and is more subservient to them / and is [full of] secret words / and is full of sad thoughts.

Cancer has the chest / ribs / spleen / and the lungs / when the Moon is in Cancer / which is a nocturnal sign / cold moist / watery and phlegmatic / and is good to walk at midnight / it is good to buy and sell / it is good to start fighting / and all things are good which have to do with water / like milling / fishing / and channelling water / it is best to take medicine as the Moon is in his house and is in his joy / which is / that a lot of moisture is available / it is beneficial to do things which will soon come to an end / but it is bad to [take] medicine for the chest / or to build a house / to move into a new house or possess one / or to work with fire / the time is moist and cold / and this is happening when this sign is rising from the orient.

Leo

The Lion is the nocturnal house of the Sun and is the iiii.[32] heavenly sign and has xix. stars / their distribution is said to be this on the head he has iii. stars and they shine brightly / [there] are iii. on the neck / ii. on the chest / one of them is very clear / and its name is Tyberoni on the spine at the end of the tail i. large and clear / under the chest ii. on the right foot of the front leg i. clear and brightly shining / and in the middle of the belly slightly towards the back legs ii. on the shoulders i. brightly shining and in the middle of the tail i. on the foot of the right hind leg i. on the knee of the left back leg i. underneath the bridle on the head i. in front of the mouth i. white clear and beautiful / its name is Dog / and is called Dog for the reason / that this star has the nature and qualities of a dog.

Who will be conceived or born under the lion in its time / will be lucky and unlucky in equal amounts / of Leo altogether and it may be said that if he

---

[32] Obviously a printing error as this should, of course, be the fifth sign.

does not die he will come to great honours and governance / he will be pious and mild / of pure and consistent disposition / he desires many things / he is strong and can jump easily / and to go into a room[33] / which continues to stay under his rule for a long time / he is wise and intelligent / very modest.

Leo has the upper part of the stomach / and the heart / the sides the back and what is missing inside them / when the Moon is in Leo / it is a strong sign and offensive / hot and dry of choleric nature / and is masculine / then it is good to talk about kings and violence and everything that wants to be achieved which is good / and all things which shall not come to an end / without these I will omit here / it is good to lay foundations of castles and houses or to move into houses / buying and exchanging money and cloth / with bright colours / it is bad to start on long journeys / and hiking / and to tailor clothes for women or putting them on / if he is getting ill in [this sign] or bad luck starts / it is bad to take or drink medicines / because they will be vomited up with blood / it is bad [to take] medicine for the liver and the heart and all internal things / if the sign is rising from the orient / it will be a warm and dry time / but if the Moon is moving across Leo it will be rainy and foggy.

Virgo

Virgo is the nocturnal house of Mercury / and is the sixth heavenly sign / and has nineteen stars / their distribution is said to be as follows / on the head he has a very dark one / its name is Poenoch / on each shoulder a bright clear one / on the top on each wing two being close together / three of them are small and dark / and the fourth is a bit bigger / and the star on the right wing near the shoulder / its name is Protrygitir / On each elbow a little one / and it is bright and clear / in the right hand one clear and large / named Spieci / therefore his hand is made of spiky ears made of corn / and her virtue is inflowing / inherent / and laudable / and therefore who will be conceived or born under him / will never be poor / in the right hand he

---

[33] *Camyn, camin,* … "chimney" or "oven" but as well "chamber".

has a little dark one / on the skirt above the knees six little dark [ones] / on each foot one star.

Who would be conceived or born under this sign / would be lucky and unlucky like a virgin in all things / therefore it has to be said / that this person naturally has to be prudish fearful / and generally ill / reputable and pure / and would easily be converted at any time / and easily believe what one is telling them / and enjoys to watch [other people] arguing / and is learning many things by heart / and enjoys viewing kingdoms and foreign countries / so that he is able to talk about it / he grieves much about other people's poverty / he is good / and remorseful / and humble in his works.

Virgo has the belly and the secret places / as the intestines / and what is surrounding [them]. When the Moon is in Virgo / which is a bi-corporeal sign lovely and of the south[34] / as well cold and dry / melancholy / feminine. It is good to plant trees / gardens and vines / and what one should do with soil / like in any other common sign / like Virgo / Sagittarius and Pisces. And it is good to do things which shall increase too / it is bad to marry a virgin / because she would be barren / and would neither give birth to sons nor children / but it is good to marry a widow. It is bad travelling in a northerly direction[35] / and undertake tasks which have to do with fire / and ingest medicines / It makes a cold and dry time and [there is] wind close to the ground / and the clouds are moving forwards and backwards / sometimes with water sometimes with little water through the air.

---

[34] *mittäglich*

[35] Reading "…travelling in a northerly direction" for "…travelling towards midnight".

Libra

Libra is the nocturnal house of Venus / and is the seventh sign / and has seven stars [note in left margin: Biginus has eight and orders them differently] / their distribution is as follows / on top of the scales are three / they are not far from each other / orderly like a proper path / and the highest [one] is smaller than all the others / but it shines brighter / and is more white in colour than the others / on each end of the scales is one / they are large and bright in the two bowls of the scales / one in each part.

Who will be conceived or born in this sign / has naturally luck and bad luck / each to the same amount / like a weight on the scales / this person will become a natural wooer and will enjoy virtue and love / and will get rid of malice / and will soon abstain from doing either / he is generally good and just / contrite and clean / honest and humble. When the Moon is in Libra in the setting sign / which is moist / airy / sanguine and masculine / it is good to wander towards the west[36] / and to buy and sell land / and to let / and to do all the things that soon need to come to an end / except the ones I exclude / It is bad to [take] medicine for the backside and the bladder / the kidneys / and all things in connection with the ground or which should be accomplished by the ground / and which shall not come to an end soon / It is [a] warm and moist time and horrid winds / and then it is good to travel / and this has to be understood of the aforementioned signs too / when the sign rises with the Sun.

Scorpio

Scorpio is the diurnal house of Mars / and is the eighth sign of heaven / and has xii. stars / their distribution is as follows / on each horn are ii. the two first ones are very clear / the other two are a bit dark / on the forehead he has two / in the mouth one / on the back three very clear stars / on the belly two.

---

[36] *occident*

Who will be conceived or born under this sign / is naturally lucky and unlucky / like the scorpion in all / and is naturally frightened / likes to be silent / and is a leader of whores / and a very evildoing person or robber / unfaithful and mean and is treacherous in his deeds.

Scorpio has power over the private parts / testicles / anus / and the bladder / over the marrow and days of sickness / deficiency and discharges from the inside. When the Moon is in Scorpio / which is a fixed sign and of the north[37] cold and moist / and watery / and phlegmatic / and feminine / it is not good to begin anything / because the Moon is in his[38] virtue and fortune[39] / but it is good to take medicine / but not to start travelling into another country / and not to climb trees and mountains / [not] to enter a ship nor take medicine for the private parts / when the sign is rising with the Sun.

Sagittarius

Sagittarius is Jupiter's nocturnal house / and is the ninth sign of heaven / and has xxii. stars / their distribution is as follows / On the head he has ii. and in the hand ii. and on the arrow ii. on the front where the iron is / on the right elbow i. on the right hand one / at the belly of the animal one / on the spine under the calf ii. on each knee at the front i. and beneath the legs vii. called the crown / on top of the arrow one brightly shining / on the fletchings ii.

Who will be conceived or born under this sign / naturally has luck and bad luck in all things / like Sagittarius / and things will come to him easily. He

---

[37] *mitternächtlich*

[38] I want to point out that in modern day German the Moon is always masculine and the Sun feminine.

[39] This is obviously an error and we can only presume that the author had Mars in mind.

is strong in his deeds / first he is frightened then he is in need[40] / he is grateful / and overcomes much / and protects[41] many things / he is unchaste / he is rich / and the people love him / and has much honour.

Sagittarius has the hips and the upper part of the thighs / When the Moon is in Sagittarius / which is a bi-corporeal sign and of the east[42] warm and dry / choleric and masculine / then it is good to have friendships and contracts made / to get married / but the wife will not be fertile with sons or boys / it is good to bathe / at rising time it is good to walk / and not to travel into another country to buy and sell / and to begin any work to do with fire / it is good to exchange money / and to start fighting / and it is bad to do things which can be done with water or with earth / like planting trees / sowing fields / medicate the thighs / this sign gives a warm and dry time.

Capricorn

Capricorn is the nocturnal house of Saturn / and is the x. sign in heaven / and has xxvii. stars / their distribution is as follows / on the top of each horn ii. and ii. on the nose which are large and clear / on the head ii. and underneath the neck one / which is large and clear / on the right foot of the front leg ii. on top of each other / and at the bottom of the same foot on top of the shoe another one / at the spine vii. at the bottom on the belly v. and at the tail one / and on the top of the tail ii.

Who will be conceived or born under this sign / has luck and bad luck in equal amounts / like a goat / but is naturally more unlucky than lucky / simple / more poor than rich / and he is not grateful for service or deeds done to him / he fears malady / if one can trust him.

---

[40] *gedurftig*

[41] Reading as *beweren* "to protect", but possibly *bewëren* "to bring something in your possession" or *bewêren* "to attempt", "to prove".

[42] *mittäglich*

Capricorn has the knees and the other joints of the knees and their illnesses / When the Moon is in Capricorn in the southern[43] sign / which is cold and dry / melancholy / feminine and earthy / it is good to be in the garden / to plant vines / it is beneficial to start the journey and walk towards midday[44] / as well as to sell and buy / and all things which shall soon come to fruition / only these are exempt / it is bad to walk towards midnight and to do things which are done with fire / it is not good to venesect[45] nor to drink [medicine] / neither to medicate the knees / and it is a cold and dry time / and the wind is close to the ground / and the clouds are moving across the sky with water [in them] / and it is generally heavily foggy and a dark time.

Aquarius

Aquarius is the nocturnal house of Saturn / and is the eleventh sign in heaven / and has xxxiii. stars / their distribution is as follows / on the head he has ii. which are dark / on each shoulder a large one / on the right elbow a small one / on the left elbow one very large and clear one / on each hand one / on each breast one / on the right leg on the top where the private parts are one / on each knee one / on the right kneecap one / on each foot one.

Who will be conceived or born under this sign / has naturally luck and bad luck equally in all things just like the water bearer and he is more unlucky than lucky / and he often suffers poverty and is sad.

Aquarius has the shinbones down to the ankles where the heel is and its joints and veins / as well as their illnesses. When the Moon is in Aquarius / which is a fixed sign and of the west[46] / warm and moist / airy / sanguine

---

[43] *mittäglich*

[44] Walking towards midday has to be read for walking in a southerly direction.

[45] *...zu lassen*.

[46] *Niedergänglich* means literally "descending" or "setting".

and male sign / it is good to start building a house / to take a housewife as a wife and bring her into your home / and it is good to venesect[47] / and good to do things which shall last / it is bad to medicate your leg and to wander / and [for] what shall end soon / the time is warm and moist / and makes good winds.

Pisces

Pisces is the nocturnal house of Jupiter / and has xxxix. stars / they are distributed as follows / The fish looking towards midday has xii stars underneath / the other fish looking towards midnight / has xv. stars in his surrounding or circle / and the rope or string which leads from one fish to the other / has xii. stars / and iii. are towards midnight / and iii. towards midday / iii. towards rising / and iii. towards setting / which is in the centre part of the string.

Who will be born or conceived under this sign / has luck and bad luck in equal parts like the sign of Pisces / he will naturally be laborious[48] / vague / good / mild and peaceful / and talks little / he is of sickly nature in his strength / he is subservient and fearful and lives a reputable life / and is grateful towards many people / but fraudulent / and is often lucky.

Pisces has the feet / their veins / and their illnesses / as periodical rheumatism in their feet / When the Moon is in Pisces / which is a bi-corporeal sign / of the north[49] / cold and moist / phlegmatic / feminine / it is good to take a housewife and make friends / exchange coins and silver / and produce weapons / and everything one wants to produce with water / as milling / culverts / and move on water towards midnight / and it is good to have a drink / and [for] buying and selling / and what shall be parted through Pisces / it is bad to treat the feet and everything else

---

[47] ...zu lassen.

[48] *weitschweifig*

[49] *mitternächtlich*

belonging to them / and what has to be done with fire / it makes a watery and moist cold time.

Sphere of the Twelve Signs and their Nature

This sphere shows the order of the signs / and what is their natural way / and shows the four places rise and set / noon and north / and which is the arch of the day and night / which is to the right side and which to the left.

Characters and Figures of the Aspects

Opposition	Has 6. signs	☍
Conjunction	In one sign	☌
△ Trine	Has 4. signs	
□ Square	Has 3. signs	
✶ Sextile	Has 2. signs	

This Sphere shows / how the Signs are Aspecting each other /

if two Planets or more are together / it is called conjunction / when they are in one sign and one degree / if a Planet is in one degree of one sign / and another Planet in the same degree of the seventh sign / this is called opposition[50]

Characters and Figures of the Planets	Character[s] of the xii. signs

---

[50] *widerstellig / oppositio / oder gegenschein*

♄ Saturn	♈ Aries
♃ Jupiter	♉ Taurus
♂ Mars	♊ Gemini
☉ Sun	♋ Cancer
♀ Venus	♌ Leo
☿ Mercury	♍ Virgo
☽ Moon	♎ Libra
	♏ Scorpio
	♐ Sagittarius
	♑ Capricorn
	♒ Aquarius
	♓ Pisces

Contrafacture and Pictures of the Heavenly Bodies / with the Fixed Stars

Images / Heavenly Pictures

These pictures are xxxvi towards the north[51] / the first one is called Little Bear / stretched out below the tail of the Dragon / the other one towards midday Ursa Major the Great Bear / which is spread towards the head of the Dragon / the third one is the Dragon in Aries / is very steady and indigent.[52] The fourth is Hercules in Sagittarius / and is very close to it. The v. is the Crown in Virgo / the vi. is Serpentarius in the middle of Scorpio / the vii. is Boetes in Virgo up to the middle of Libra / the viii. is Ophiochus or Agitator at the end of Taurus and the beginning of Gemini / the horse in Cancer / and a little bit in the beginning of Leo. The ix. is Cephus in the beginning of Aquarius / the x. is Cassiopeia at the back of Pisces and Arione / the xi. is Pegasus / that is the higher horse in Capricorn / the xii. is Andromeda in the first fish of the sign of Pisces near Aquarius / the xiii. is Perseus in the middle of Aries / and through the whole of the head of Taurus / the xiiii. is Triangle below Pisces and Aries / the xv. is Clota at the end of Taurus / xvi. is Lyra in the head of Capricorn / the xvii. is Cygnus in the last part of Capricorn and the first part of Aquarius / the xviii. is the flying Hawk in Sagittarius and Capricorn / Aries and Pisces / the xx. is Cetus stretched out under Aquarius and Capricorn / the xxi. is Eridanus or Millus in Aquarius and Pisces / the xxii. is Delphinus below Sagittarius and Capricorn / the xxiii. is Orion below Aries and Taurus / the xxiiii. is Canis which is Syrion between Cancer and Leo / the xxv. is Lepus or hare / between Taurus and Gemini / the xxvi. is Argo the ship / between Cancer and Leo / the xxvii. is Astronothus in Scorpio / the xxviii. is Demon meridianus / is more in Cancer than in Capricorn / and splits the heaven in half / the xix. is the great fish between Aquarius and Pisces / the xxx. is Puteus and lies in the depth of the tail of Scorpio / the xxxi. is Centaurus at

---

[51] Ibid.

[52] *gedürftig*

the end of Libra and the beginning of Scorpio / the xxxii. is Hydra in the middle of Leo / through the whole of Virgo and the first half of Libra / the xxxiii. is Canis minor the little dog [which] is between Capricorn and Aquarius who is called Anticanis or Thion by another name / the xxxiiii. [is] Equs secundus[53] or the other horse / [which] is between Gemini and Cancer / the xxxv. is Cerabellu[54] the drill is at the tail of Sagittarius and the tail of Capricorn / the xxxvi. is Vexillum[55] a flag / one part is in Leo and one part in Virgo / at the beginning of Virgo.

Of the Fixed Stars and their Qualities

Every reader may receive the art and message of the xxxvi. signs or pictures or figures / in the sky or on Earth / [how] to extract a judgement[56] of things / through an example and true simile to this here present in this place / therefore we lay down through figures the xxxvi. images / which are pictures or figures / as they are dissected in the sky.

The Great Bear

Ursa Major, the Great Bear / is a figure or a heavenly image / and is very close to the head of the Dragon / this bear is called Arcturus / and has many stars / amongst which are xxiii. one can see / their distribution is as follows / on his head there are vii. which build a cart / and it is said that there are iiii. stars for the four wheels / and ii. stars for the cattle / and one

---

[53] Equus secundus.

[54] Terebellum, Omega Sagittarius.

[55] The word Vela comes from the Indo-European root *weg - 'To weave a web'. Suffixed form *weg-slo-; veil, Vela (sails, plural of velum), velarium, velum (sail), vexilum (a flag, banner, or ensign. The weblike part of a feather; the vane), voile (a fabric of plain weave used especially for making dresses and curtains), reveal, revelation, (these words from Latin velum, 'a sail, curtain, veil').

[56] *iudicium*

star for the shaft / on each of the axles he has a little and a bit dark one / on each shoulder ii. on the chest i. on the front of the right foot ii. which are shining strongly and are clear / and on top of the tail a clear one / on the belly i. on the spine i. on the back of the kneecap ii. on top of the foot ii. small ones on the top of the tail iii. / which go back on to the foot.

Who will be conceived or born under the Great Bear / if he does not die / he will be great and mighty in the world / and he will rule over many people / and many people will follow him / many people will have great hope and trust in him / and it indicates a good and long life in the world / and he will have many blessings, honour and worthiness in great peace.

The Little Bear

Ursa Minor, the Little Bear, is a figure or heavenly image / which is close to the tail of the Dragon / and is wrought around by the tail of the Dragon / these stars are given many names / and [he] is so virtuous / that he shows sailors at sea their way / because with his advice and leadership / ships may come and go / and will be led expertly / this Little Bear and the other one who is larger / are called Arctura[57] / or Actophylax / or Elix[58] / or Polus Arcticus[59] / and in himself he has many stars / their distribution is as follows / at the axles he has a star which is clear and pure / on the belly i. on the spine i. at the chest one / and iiii. stars are building the cart or wagon

---

[57] FSC p139 from Arktouros, the Bear Guard. Also called Arctophilax, the Bear Watcher. Influence: According to Ptolemy it is of the nature of Mars and Jupiter, but Alvidas substitutes Venus and Mercury conjoined. It gives riches, honours, high renown, self-determination and prosperity by navigation and voyages. If rising: good fortune with many cares and anxieties through own folly.

[58] Perhaps after the Greek word "helix", to be curved or to spiral.

[59] FSC p184f Polaris, influence: of the nature of Saturn and Venus. It causes much sickness, trouble, loss of fortune, disgrace and great affliction...

/ above the tail there are ii. they stand a little apart from those two / and the ii. stars are for the ii. cattle / and the third for the shaft.

Who will be conceived or born under the Little Bear / will become great in the world / which may be secular or clerical / and his whole family will enjoy his riches.

The Dragon in Aries and in Scorpio

Draco the Dragon is a heavenly image / and has xv. stars / their distribution is as follows / on the forehead he has three stars[60] / which are in one line / and they are small / and there are xii. other stars and they are equal in size and width / and the stars are a bit separated from each other.

Who will be conceived or born under this sign Draco / will be an evil person in nature / and he will be unfaithful and a leader of whores / and is poor[61] and disreputable / and likes to fight / and is full of lies / and likes to be angry and unpleasant / and denies easily / and is a gatherer of corn / a thief and a murderer / and is wise and full of good thoughts / and is sometimes verbose[62] / and is more poor than rich.

Hercules or Eugonasin[63] in Sagittarius

---

[60] SH p76 Two of the three stars are β – Rastaban (means "serpent's head") and γ – Eltanin (Arabic for "Dragon's head"). I could not identify the third star so far. FSC p194 Rastaban, influence: of the nature of Saturn and Mars. It gives loss of property, violence, criminal inclinations and accidents.

[61] *gedürftig*

[62] *weitschweiffig*

[63] Manilius: *Astronomica*, p353: "Hercules, the figure on bended knee and called by the Greek name of Engonasin, about whose origin no certainty prevails. Of this constellation is begotten the desertion, craftiness, and deceit characteristic of its children, and from it comes the thug who terrorizes the heart of the city. If perchance his mind is moved to consider a profession,

I am daring / unchaste / strong / My heart is longing for many riches. My children settle for poverty / And they are cheerful on their path.

Hercules is a heavenly image / and has xxii. stars / their layout is / like the tree bearing golden apples / on its head there is one star / which is shining bright[64] / on each shoulder i. that shines bright / one on the left elbow / on the left hand i. on the right hand one / one on the left breast / on the right breast ii. on the right thigh ii. on the right knee one / on the right shin one / on the right foot one / on the left shin ii. on the left foot one / one big and bright one on the brow of the lion / on the neck and hair of the lion four / on the sword one.

Who will be born or conceived under this sign / will be poor[65] by nature / strong and unchaste / more poor than rich / and will do damage to another one easily / he is grateful / overcomes much / his heart desires to do many things / he will be industrious[66] / and is restless too.

The Crown in Virgo and Libra

Corona is a heavenly image / and has ix. stars in its circumference / their distribution is as follows / at the bottom of the crown is a gemstone in the

---

Engonasin will inspire him with enthusiasm for risky callings, with danger the price, for which he will sell his talents: daring narrow steps on a path without thickness, he will plant firm feet on a horizontal tightrope; then, as he attempts an upward route to heaven, (on a sloping tightrope) he will all but lose his footing and, suspended in mid-air, he will keep a multitude in suspense upon himself."

[64] SH p76 α – Ras Algethi (Arabic for "head of the kneeler") is one of the largest stars known.

[65] *gedurftig*

[66] *weitschweiffig*

shape of a square / therein is one star[67] / and the other stars are surrounding the crown.

Who is born or conceived under this sign / will be naturally pale in face and body / and clean with his clothes and honest / and will be rich and [will own] many things / and will have a good life / and he will come to honours and worthiness too / and many people will like him.

Serpentarius in Scorpio

Serpentarius is the name given to me. My children will live in fear and poverty / They will die of poison / or die of a poisoned worm.

Serpentarius or Ophiuchus[68] is a heavenly image / some call it Asclepius / and has xvii. stars / and the serpent around the human has xix. their distribution is as follows / The man Serpentario has one large star on his head[69] / and it is clear and large / on each shoulder [is] one / on the left hand iii. on the right hand are iiii. and ii. are below the four which are bigger and brighter than the other two / a little one on each side of the genitals / a large, bright one on the right shinbone / a small one on each foot / but those two are clear. The picture of the serpent has xxv. stars / their distribution is as follows / the serpent has one in its mouth / and one in the nostrils / four on the first bend / there are eight on the other bend /

---

[67] FSC p131f Alphecca ... a brilliant white star in the knot of the ribbon ... according to Ptolemy it is of the nature of Venus and Mercury ... it gives honour, dignity and poetical and artistic ability.

[68] Manilius: *Astronomica*, book1, p31: Ophiuchus means 'he who holds the serpent' and that is how he is depicted. The struggle will last forever, since they wage it on equal terms with equal powers.

[69] SH p90 α – Ras Alhague, from the Arabic for "head of the serpent-charmer". Hoffmann / Ebertin: *Die Bedeutung der Fixsterne*, p57: ... especially infections and poisoning.

six on the third bend / on the fourth bend a hook[70] like a circle or round / there are five up to the end of the tail.

Boetes or Arcturus in Virgo and Libra

Boetes or Arcturus[71] is a heavenly image / and has xxi. stars / their distribution is as follows / at each shoulder i. at the right hand iiii. / on each breast i. small and rather dark / at the right elbow i. rather clear / below each knee i. being large and clear / at each foot i. at the sickle iiii. in the right hand / at the pike or lance in the left hand iii. one in the middle and the other ii. both on one end of the pike or lance.

Who is conceived or born under this sign / always lives for work / and more in poverty than in riches / and does nothing else but farmer's things[72] / and seems impoverished in his works.

The Charioteer[73] in Taurus and Gemini

Agitator is my name / A leisurely lifestyle annoys me / My children work with the plough / they never get enough to eat and drink.

---

[70] Here in the original text the German word *gond* is used. According to J. G. Krünitz, *Oekonomische Encyklopädie*, 1773 – 1858, this word is related to a door hinge, particularly the strong hook whereupon the door is hung.

[71] SH p48 α – Arcturus, ... the name means "bear-keeper", referring to Boötes' perpetual pursuit of Ursa Major and Ursa Minor (the Greater and Lesser Bears) around the North Pole.

[72] SH p48 β – Nekkar, the name derives from the Arabic for "Ox-driver", a name also given to the whole constellation.

[73] FSC p31 Auriga, the Charioteer ... Influence. According to Ptolemy the bright stars are like Mars and Mercury. ... The native is fond of country life and may be a teacher or have the upbringing of young people.

Agitator the Carter / is a heavenly image / has thirteen stars / their distribution is as follows / On the head he has one / on each shoulder one / but[74] the one in the left shoulder is larger and shines brighter / and is called Capra[75] / one in the right hand / and one in the left hand / at each knee one / at the mouth of the first horse one / at the ears of the other horse one / on the head of the right oxen one / on the right foot of the first horse one / on the right foot of the other bull one.

Who will be conceived or born under this sign / likes to do as the farmers always tend to do in their villages to work all the time / cattle and wood and ploughing / and lives more for his work than for a rest / and is more poor than rich / more good things will come to him in his youth than in his old age / but he will be rich if he gets old.

Cepheus in Aquarius and Taurus

Cepheus is my name / My children are wealthy / Their lives consists of work / They do not long for great honours / They do not like to take on many duties / and enjoy being idle.

Cepheus is a heavenly image / and has many stars / and their distribution is as follows / on the head he has two / very large and shining bright / on each shoulder one / on each elbow one small and dark / in each hand a clear one / on the belt three / on the sword strap are seven / on the right thigh one / on the left knee two / on the right foot two / on the left foot three / one is in the same spot[76] on the same foot / the other two are slightly remote of him.

---

[74] These are Capella and Menkalinan. SH p46 β – Menkalinan, the name of the star derives from the Arabic for "charioteer's left shoulder".

[75] SH p46 α – Capella, the name means "she-goat". This is the sixth brightest star in the sky.

[76] *punten*

Who will be conceived or born in this sign[77] / will always be more rich than poor / and owns many items / and lives more in peace than at work / but he will not achieve honours or worthiness or government / but may be drinking well / eating / and is idle and unchaste.

Cassiopeia in Pisces and Aries

Cassiopeia is my name / The faces of my children are beautiful / They are keen and unchaste / They will endure a nasty death.

Cassiopeia is a heavenly image / and has xiiii. stars / their distribution is as follows / on the head she has a large and bright one / on each shoulder a clear one / on the right breast a clear one[78] / and on each hand a large and bright one[79] / and one on the navel / on the left hip two / on the left knee a bright one / on top of the chair two bright ones.

Who will be born or conceived under this sign[80] / will have a pretty face / and is unchaste / wants for many things[81] / rich and full of joy / and has a

---

[77] Manilius, *Astronomica,* book 5 p336: Cepheus will not engender dispositions inclined to sport. He fashions faces marked by a stern demeanour, and moulds a countenance whereon is depicted gravity of mind. Such men will live on worry and will incessantly recall the traditions of a bygone age and commend old Cato's maxims. FSC p37 According to Ptolemy Cepheus is like Saturn and Jupiter.

[78] SH p60 α – Schedar, the name for this star means breast. Hoffmann / Ebertin: *Die Bedeutung der Fixsterne,* p18: Schedir, main star alpha of Cassiopeia is of the nature of Saturn which is mitigated by Venus. This star is synonymous with seriousness and joy of life.

[79] Only Caph in SH p60 β – Caph, the name derives from the Arabic title for the constellation.

[80] FSC p36 Influence: according to Ptolemy this constellation is of the nature of Saturn and Venus.

[81] *gedürftig*

charmed life / until his life will come to an end / but he will die an evil death / which is / either he will be murdered / or his throat will be cut / or [he] will perish in a violent storm.

Pegasus in Capricorn and Pisces

Alferas[82] or Pegasus or Equus Vespertinus the evening horse / it is a heavenly image / and has xxii. stars / their distribution is as follows / on the head a clear [one] / and on top by the ears on each ear a bright one / below the face two clear ones / on the neck iiii. on the two cheeks ii. on the right shoulder of the right wing one / in the middle of the wing one / on top of the feathers of the right wing one / on the right shoulder one / on the chest one / on the spine one / on the navel one which is large and clear / on each knee one / on each nail of the foot one.

Who will be born or conceived under this sign / will be copious / wants for many things[83] / full of joy / rich / and is lucky / and he is unchaste / and is servant to another / and is honest / and reputable / and knows how to flatter / and does not make many words / and if he does not die / he will achieve great honours or worthiness or appointments.

Andromeda in Pisces and Aries

My name is Andromeda / Women I do not apprehend / My children commit heresy / Therefore they do not live long / They are able to flatter, too / And are full of negative virtues.

---

[82] SH p94 a - Andromedae – Alpheratz, … once δ Peg, it was also known under the name Sirrah ("navel"), marking the navel of the horse.

[83] *gedürftig*

Andromeda is a heavenly image / and has xx. stars / their distribution is as follows / on the head there is a mighty and clear one[84] / and on each shoulder a small one / and on each elbow a small one / in the right hand a very clear one / in the left hand one / on the right arm ii. very clear [ones] / on the belt three[85] / after the alignment of Libra / at the front end of the coat iii. below the coat on each knee one shining brightly / on the right foot ii. on the left foot one.

Who will be born or conceived under the sign[86] / will become rich in his days / and has a cheerful face and [is] pretty / he is lucky / and unchaste with heresy / and flatters / and is wise / and is serving another / and believes what he is told / and asks people humbly what he wants to ask them / and creates much harm / and receives much harm / because he has to die / and loses his possessions.

Perseus in Aries and Taurus

---

[84] SH p38 α – Alpheratz or Sirrah both its common names are derived from the same Arabic phrase, Al Surrat al Faras, "the navel of the horse", as this star was at one time considered part of Pegasus (δ Peg.).

FSC p133 Alpheratz, influence: According to Ptolemy it is of the nature of Jupiter and Venus, and to these Alvidas adds Mars also. It gives independence, freedom, love, riches, honour and a keen intellect.

[85] SH p38 β – Mirach, the name is derived from the Arabic "girdle". FSC p178 Mirach, influence: According to Ptolemy it is of the nature of Venus; and, to Alvidas, of Mars and the Moon. It give personal beauty, a brilliant mind, a love of home, great devotion, beneficence, forgiveness, love, overcoming by kindness, renown and good fortune in marriage.

[86] FSC p26 Andromeda, influence: According to Ptolemy the influence of this constellation is similar to that of Venus, though the legend would lead one to suppose some connection with Virgo. It is said to bestow purity of thought, virtue, honour and dignity upon its natives, but to cause battle with chimerical fears and a tendency to become easily discouraged.

I, Perseus, am wild and full of joy / And joyfully maintain secret courtly love / My children will become very rich / but they have to die by the sword.

Perseus is a heavenly image / and has xviii. stars / their distribution is as follows / on the head he has a clear one / on the right hand one / on the right elbow one / on the left hand one / on the right side near the genitals a clear one / on the right breast one / on each knee one / on each shin one / on each foot one / on the sword one / on the Gorgon's head which is chopped off[87] / are iiii.

Who will be born or conceived under this sign[88] / he will be hard working[89] and rich / apt and unchaste / wants for many things[90] and [is] strong / of a sure heart / and is lucky / and likes to have many riches and wants them for himself / and is wealthy and owes many things / and resembles an evil and bewitched person / and creates much falsity amongst people / and dies an evil death / being stabbed with swords / or with other knives or pikes.

The Triangle Pisces and Aries as well as in Taurus

Triangulus is a heavenly image / and has iii. stars / their distribution is as follows / in each angle is a large and bright star.

---

[87] SH p96 β – Algol, the demon-star, literally "the ghoul"... this star has widely been regarded as the most malevolent in the sky. FSC p124 Algol, influence: Of the nature of Saturn and Jupiter. It causes misfortune, violence, decapitation, electrocution and mob violence and gives a dogged and violent nature that causes death to the native or others.

[88] FSC p56 Perseus, influence: according to Ptolemy, Perseus is like Jupiter and Saturn. It is said to give an intelligent, strong, bold and adventurous nature, but a tendency to lying.

[89] *weitschweiffig*

[90] *gedürftig*

Who will be born or conceived under this sign[91] / will suffer an unfortunate life / and therefore he is more poor than rich / and attains great honours / but they will not last long.

The Mother Hen with her Chicks in Taurus

Gallina[92] or Clotha is a heavenly image / and has vii. stars / one star is smaller than the others / and therefore they are not equal they contain the order of two ways / their distribution is as follows / six are shining close to each other / and between the two paths is one which is small and dark.

Who will be conceived or born under this sign / until he dies / will receive many honours and dignities / and many riches / and more so if he gets older / than in his youth / he will be wise too / and likes to sing / and is full of sense and wants many things[93] / and his wisdom is of use / and the people appreciate him.

Lyra in Capricorn

Lyra is a heavenly image / and has xi. stars / their distribution is as follows / on top on the two horns on each horn one / on each shoulder one / deep below one / on each side next to the attachment one / in the middle of the strings or cords one / one each side at the bottom where the cords are one / and on top of the strings one.

---

[91] FSC p64 Triangulum, influence: According to Ptolemy it is like Mercury. It is said to give a just, companionable, truthful, righteous and benevolent nature, …

[92] *Gallina*, from the Latin for "domestic hen". This constellation may be what became in 1592 known as Columba, the Dove.

[93] *gedürftig*

Who will be born or conceived under this sign[94] / likes to listen to songs and to harps being played / lyres and all string music / and likes to see [people] joking and reprimanding / and is joyful and ingenious / and is more poor than rich / and has the luck of a liar.

The Swan in Capricorn and Aquarius

Cignus or the Swan is a heavenly image and has xv. stars / his distribution is as follows / on the head he has one large shining star[95] / on the body a shining one / on the right wing v. one after the other / on the chest one / on the tail one / below the feet one / and on the left wing v. too.

Who will be born or conceived under this sign[96] / will be very lucky / and bad luck comes to him easily / and leaves him soon again / he likes to catch birds and to fish / and likes to grab the large ones instead of the small ones / he will be more poor than rich / he is verbose[97] and a little naïve.

The Flying Eagle or Hawk in Sagittarius and Capricorn

---

[94] FSC p51 Influence: According to Ptolemy Lyra is like Venus and Mercury. It is said to give an harmonious, poetical and developed nature, fond of music and apt in science and art, but inclined to theft.

[95] SH p74 β – Albireo the name comes from a 16th century mistranslation of the Arabic. FSC p118f Albireo, influence: Of the nature of Venus and Mercury. It gives a handsome appearance, neatness, a lovable disposition and beneficience in despair.

[96] FSC p42 Cygnus, influence: C. gives a contemplative, dreamy, cultured and adaptable nature. … There is some love of water and swimming and the arts.

[97] *weitschweiffig*

Vultur volans[98] is a heavenly image / and has v. stars / their distribution is as follows / on the head there is one which is very clear and very large[99] / below the beak two / on the chest one / on the right foot one / on the arrow four.

Who will be conceived or born under this sign / will be verbose[100] by nature and unsettled / and much lying / he is poor[101] / and unchaste / childish / a gambler / more poor than rich / and is still lucky all the time / and luck comes to him easily / but he does not recognise the gift of luck / and he thinks that it is not enough what happens to him or becomes of him / if she is female so she will be a prostitute who is open about it / and will be laborious[102] / and thankful / and she will receive many goods.

The descending Eagle in Pisces and Aries

Vultur cadens[103] is a heavenly image and has iiii. stars / they are distributed as follows / on the head he has a large clear one[104] / on each wing one / on

---

[98] FSC p29 Aquila, legend: Originally called Vulture Volans or the Flying Grype ... Influence: According to Ptolemy the influence of Aquila is similar to that of Mars and Jupiter. It is said to give great imagination, strong passions, indomitable will, a dominating character, influence over others, clairvoyance, a keen penetrating mind and ability for chemical research.

[99] SH p42 α – Altair, takes its name from the Arabic word for eagle ...

[100] *weitschweiffig*

[101] *gedürftig*

[102] *weitschweiffig*

[103] This is another name for Lyra FSC p50 Lyra: After Orpheus was slain by the Thracian women, Jupiter placed the lyre in heaven at the request of Apollo and the Muses. This constellation was often called Vultur Cadens, or the Falling Grype by the ancients.

the chest a small dark one / his arrow has iiii. stars / one is on the iron / another one is on the shaft / the other two [are] on the feathers.

Who will be conceived or born under this sign / if it will be a man he will be a mocker and liar / poor[105] and a drunkard / and [he] will be a knave and a murderer / and is rude / and is still lucky / and he does not recognise it / and he is not picking it up / and what he picks up he does not keep for long / and therefore he is called fickle and unsettled[106] / and more rich than poor in all his life / and if it will be a woman / she will be like him and unsettled[107] / and fickle / and lazy / and likes to lie / and will be an unchaste whore / and will lead a shameless life / and is poor in property[108] / and will get many lucky things / and will not ever have enough of them.

The Whale in Capricorn and Aquarius as well as in Taurus

Cetus or Balena[109] is a heavenly image / and has xxii. stars / their distribution is as follows / in front on the nose of the fish one / on the

---

[104] SH p89 Lyra α – Vega, the fifth brightest star in the heavens … Its name derives from the Arabic for "swooping vulture (or eagle)"; to the Arabs Lyra was a bird with half-closed wings, thought to derive from ancient Indian star-lore. FSC p216f Wega, often incorrectly spelled Vega, influence: According to Ptolemy it is of the nature of Venus and Mercury; and, to Alvidas, of Saturn in trine to Jupiter from the earthy signs especially Capricorn and Taurus. It gives beneficence, ideality, hopefulness, refinement and changeability, and makes its natives grave, sober, outwardly pretentious and usually lascivious.

[105] *gedürftig*

[106] *weitschweiffig*

[107] Ibid.

[108] Reading "property" for "land".

[109] From the Italian *balaena*, baleen whales are of the genus Balaena mysticetus.

forehead one / on each wing one / on the tail v. three are small / and dark / and at the bottom of the belly are six / above the back[110] of the tail six.

Who is conceived or born under him[111] / naturally likes to fish in the sea / likes to live by the sea / and the fruit that comes from the water / and it is by the sea where he will be harmed / and [he] will be more poor than rich.

Below Cetus there is the figure of a naked human being / and has xvii. stars / their distribution is as follows / on the head there are vii. / in a circle / on his right arm which is stretched out are v. / on the backside one / on the right knee one / on the right hip one.

Who is conceived or born under this sign / he lives in terror and fear all the time / [and fears] damage and work.

The Minstrel in Aquarius and Pisces

Eridanus[112] or Joculato[113] is a heavenly image / and has xvii. stars / their distribution is as follows / on the forehead he has two / one on the throat / on the left shoulder one / on the zither iiii. / one on each end / on top of the chair and on the right side one / on the left side of the chair ii.

---

[110] *Bühel,* from Old High German *buhil,* for "hill", "hillock", the part that rises up from the head presumably, so the back.

[111] FSC p38 Cetus, influence: According to Ptolemy this constellation is like Saturn. It is said to cause laziness and idleness, but to confer an emotional and charitable nature, with ability to command.

[112] FSC 44 Eridanus, the River … Influence: according to Ptolemy all the stars with the exception of Achernar are like Saturn. Eridanus gives a love of knowledge and science, much travel and many changes, a position of authority, but danger of accidents, especially at sea, and of drowning.

[113] The constellation of Orion was sometimes called Jugula.

Who will be conceived or born under this sign / will always lead a happy life / and likes to play stringed instruments / and is more poor than rich / and will still be well looked after.

The Dolphin in Sagittarius and Capricorn as well as in Aquarius

Delphinus is a heavenly image / and has ix. stars / their distribution is as follows / in his mouth he has one and on his forehead ii. / on the feathers iii. and two next to the tail on top of the feathers / and the other one at the bottom of the feathers / on the spine one / at the rear next to the tail one.

Who will be born or conceived under this sign[114] / likes to joke / and is verbose[115] / and likes to hear new stories / and is a great traveller / and is more poor than rich / and most of his life without work / he will not know much / but will still know about a few things.

Orion between Aries and Taurus

Orion is a heavenly image / and has xvii. stars / their distribution is as follows / on the head he has iii. stars / and the middle [one] is a bit brighter than the other ii. / and on each shoulder one brightly shining[116] / on the

---

[114] FSC p42f Delphinus, influence: According to Ptolemy D. is like Saturn and Mars. It gives a simple appearance, cheerfulness, dissembling and duplicity, love of hunting and sport in general but little happiness. There is fondness for pleasure, ecclesiastical matters and travel, but danger of suffering from ingratitude.

[115] *weitschweiffig*

[116] SH p92 α – Betelgeuse, ... its name, rather prosaically, derives from the Arabic for "armpit of the central one". FSC p147 Betelgeuse, influence: According to Ptolemy it is of the nature of Mars and Mercury; and, to Alvidas, of Mercury, Saturn and Jupiter in good aspect. It gives martial honour, preferment ad wealth. SH p92 γ – Bellatrix, the name means "female warrior", which derives from a rather loose medieval translation of the Arabic Al Najiad, meaning "the conqueror". FSC p145 Bellatrix,

right elbow a small and dark one / on the right hand one / on the belt iii. on the sword ii. on each knee one / on each foot one.

Who will be conceived or born under this sign[117] / will be rich [and] wise / full of wishes[118] and strong / and likes to harm people / and likes to wear weapons and armour / and likes to kill people / and burns houses / and will receive much harm in his life / and [his] life is more uncertain than certain.

Canis Sirion dog is between Cancer and Leo

Canis or Sirion is a heavenly image and has xx. stars / their distribution is as follows / on the head is a very bright and clear one[119] / on the neck ii. on each shoulder one / they are small and dark / on the chest ii. on the front of the left foot iii. on the back of the right foot one very clear / on the spine iii. on the belly ii. close together / and on the back of the left foot one / and one on the tail.

---

influence: According to Ptolemy it is like Mars and Mercury; and to Alvidas, Mercury and Mars in good aspect. It gives great civil or military honour but danger of sudden dishonour, renown, wealth, eminent friends and liability to accidents causing blindness and ruin....

[117] FSC p55 Orion, influence: According to Ptolemy the bright stars with the exception of Betelgeuze and Bellatrix are like Jupiter and Saturn. It is said to give a strong and dignified nature, self-confidence, inconstancy, arrogance, violence, impiety, prosperity in trade and particularly by voyages or abroad, but danger of treachery and poison.

[118] *gedürftig*

[119] SH p52 α – Sirius, the name means "scorching". The brightest star in the heavens,... FSC p208 Sirius, influence: According to Ptolemy it is of the nature of Jupiter and Mars; and, to Alvidas, of the Moon, Jupiter and Mars. It gives honour, renown, wealth, ardour, faithfulness, devotion, passion and resentment, and makes its natives custodians, curators and guardians....

Who will be born or conceived under this sign[120] / will be hateful and warmongering / and worthless / and likes to shout / and is true to his friends / and is inquisitive about other people's goods / and is verbose[121] / and is more poor than rich / and lives more to be lazy / than to work.

Lepus the Hare is between Taurus and Gemini

Lepus is a heavenly image / and has vii. stars / their distribution is as follows / on each ear is one / on the chest two / on the back a quite bright and large one / and on the back of each foot one.

Who will be born or conceived under this sign[122] / will always be poor and fearful / and will have a quiet life / laborious[123] / unfortunate / he will be in many places.

Argo the Ship between Cancer and Leo

Navis the ship is a heavenly image / and has xxvi. stars / their distribution is as follows / on top of the mast iii.[124] at the back of the ship on the tiller[125]

---

[120] FSC p34 Canis Major, influence: Ptolemy states that the stars of this constellation, with the exception of Sirius, are like Venus. It is said to give good qualities, charity and a faithful heart, but violent and dangerous passions.

[121] *weitschweiffig*

[122] FSC p49 Lepus, influence: According to Ptolemy, Lepus is like Saturn and Mercury. It gives quick wit, timidity, circumspection, fecundity and defiance.

[123] *weitschweiffig*

[124] Referred to later in the text as Malus, or Mast (nowadays Pyxis Nautica).

[125] *Terschen* ... meaning of the word is unclear although there might be a connection with the Latin word for tiller, 'telarium'. Probably Puppis, the stern of Argo Navis.

iii. bright ones / on one oar are v. nearly dark and small / on top between each oar one which makes iiii. and below v. one between each oar. There exists another picture called Testudo / and has iiii. stars / nearly dark and invisible.

Who will be conceived or born under this sign / will be more poor than rich / and will be longing to be a sailor or mariner / and sail on the ocean / and live off the fruit of his labour / the sea / and will visit many kingdoms and countries / maybe he will lose the shores of the [home]land / maybe he will keep it.

Astronothus is in Sagittarius and in Scorpio

Astronothus[126] is a heavenly image / and has xx. stars / their distribution is as follows / on the head he has vii. very dark / on the right hip one very dark / on the chest a clear one / on the front of the right side of the right foot a dark one / on the left thigh a bright one / on the backside two shining [ones] / on the back on the left side of the left foot two dark [ones] / on the tail two dark [ones].

Who will be conceived or born under this sign / will be naturally pretty and lucky / good and mild and peaceful / and will be rich / and will be loved by all people / and will receive great honours / and praise and worthiness if he lives / and will never turn / and is doing good things to everybody / and harms nobody / but some things he will never learn and this makes him tired / or it will take a long time.

Daemon Meridianus in Cancer and Capricorn

---

[126] Known to us as Centaurus. See as well the appropriate entry below.

Arctophilax[127] am I / and I walk in foreign lands / My children have no courage / In poverty they will be buried.

Daemon meridianus is a heavenly image / and has vii. stars / their distribution is not recorded anywhere / it may be the milky way in the sky.

Who will be born or conceived under this sign[128] / will always be very poor / and is ill and unlucky.

The Great Fish is between Aquarius and Pisces

Piscis magnus[129] is a heavenly image / it has xvi. stars / their distribution is as follows / the large fish has xii. stars / and the small [one] iiii. / the large fish's distribution is as follows / he has one in his mouth / on the forehead one / on the back iii. they are far apart from each other / under the beard one / under the belly iiii. / on the tail ii. The distribution of the little fish is as follows / on the fish's ears are ii. quite clear / on the back above the tail are ii. nearly dark.

Who will be conceived or born under this sign[130] / wants to go fishing all the time / he will be verbose[131] and quiet / and he buys and sells fish /

---

[127] A. is the Greek title for Boötes. Nevertheless, the positioning of this constellation between Cancer and Capricorn shows that it cannot be brought in connection with the real constellation Boötes.

[128] FSC p32 Boötes, the Herdsman ... influence: According to Ptolemy the influence of the constellation is like that of Mercury and Saturn, though the star Arcturus is like Mars and Jupiter. It is said to give prosperity from work, strong desires, a tendency to excess, and fondness for rural pursuits, together with some liking for occultism.

[129] Known to us as Piscis Austrinis or Piscis Australis.

[130] FSC p57f Piscis Australis ... influence: Ptolemy gives no separate influence and only describes Fomalhaut but according to Bayer the constellation is of the nature of Saturn. It is said to have an influence similar to that of Pisces, but, in addition, to augment the fortunes.

making a living from the fruit of the sea / he will never be rich / he is peaceful and quiet / does not eat much.

The Well[132] is at the end of Scorpio

Puteus otherwise called Sacrarius[133] is a heavenly image / and has iiii. stars / their distribution is as follows / on top in the flames are ii stars / a little below the mouth of the flames[134] ii. as well.

Who is born or conceived under this sign[135] / will be more poor than rich / and he will always want to make experiments in the art / so that women will adore him / or want to hear him sing / will conjure up devils / and master them / and likes to work with many metals / which is alchemy / and will be a famous person / and knowledgeable and wise / ill and full of fear.

Centaurus is between Libra and Scorpio

Centaurus is my name / My children have strong hands / Keen and unchaste they are / Subtle / fast as the wind / They like to eat and drink good things / They like to give good advice.

Centaurus is a heavenly image / and has xxiiii. stars / their distribution is as follows / on the head he has iii. small and dark / on each shoulder one clear one / on the right elbow one / in the right hand one / on the chest one

---

[131] *weitschweiffig*

[132] *Bron* or *bronn*, from Old High German *prunno*, a "well".

[133] Known to us as Ara, the Altar.

[134] The word used in the original text is *bornen*, which the Rheinische Wörterbuch translates as *brennen*, "to burn".

[135] FSC p29f Ara … influence: According to Ptolemy its influence is similar to that of Venus and also Mercury in some degree. It is said to give aptness in science, egoism, devotion and a love of ecclesiastical matters.

/ on the spine ii. and the belly ii. on the right thigh one bright shining one[136] / on the tail ii. on the back of the knee one / on each front leg one / on the front of each foot one / The distribution amongst the hare or animal in his hand is as follows / there are x. stars / on the head ii. there is one larger and clearer than the other / on the spine one shining / on the tail ii. on top of the back left foot one which is shining / on the right front foot a clear one.

Who will be born or conceived under this sign[137] / will be naturally strong / in need of many things[138] and unchaste / likes to give quickly / and is ingenious and lucky / and likes to catch venison and wild animals / and he likes to live tenderly / with good food and drink / and clothes and weapons / and he will be more rich than poor / and likes to be a servant to other people / and if he does not die he will come to great honours / as in office or other worthiness / and does not harm anybody who acts wisely / and is mild / worthy and good / and confident too.

Hydra is in the Centre of Leo through Virgo to the End of Libra

Hydra is a heavenly image / and has xlvi. stars / their distribution is as follows / on the head of the water snake are iii. and on the first bend of the snake are vi. stars / it is a little dark and small / on the other bend are iii. on the third bend are iiii. on the fourth turn ii. on the fifth up to the tail are viii.

---

[136] SH p64 α – Rigil Kentaurus or Toliman … the third brightest star in the sky. FSC p148f Bungula … according to Bullinger it bore the ancient name Toliman … influence: According to Ptolemy it is of the nature of Venus and Jupiter; and, to Alvidas, of Mars with the Moon … it gives beneficence, friends, refinement and a position of honour.

[137] FSC p37 Centaurus, influence: According to Ptolemy the stars in the human part of the figure are of the nature of Venus and Mercury, and the bright stars in the horse's part are of Venus and Jupiter. It is said to give hard-heartedness, inclination to vengeance, love of arms, strong passions and an energetic nature. It may also be connected with poison.

[138] *gedürftig*

shining ones / on top of the hare are ii. and on the neck of the hare are ii. dark [ones] / on each side are iii. at the bottom of the hare are ii. on the head of raven is a large and clear one / on the back he has ii. on the bottom of the wing where they are crossed over / there are ii. on each foot one.

Who will be conceived or born under this sign[139] / will be naturally lucky and will have many good things / but he will undo all the good through folly / and this is why he will suffer much poverty / and he will be lazy and ill / and does not acknowledge the office offered to him.

Canis Major[140] is between Capricorn and Aquarius

Prokyon or Anticanis is a heavenly image / and has many stars / amongst them are iiii. brightly shining ones / their distribution is as follows / on the neck is a clear and brightly shining one / on the chest is one nearly bright / on the two on the front joints on the shoulders on both sides a bright one / but the one which is on the neck is larger than the other stars.

Who will be conceived or born under this sign[141] / will always be faithful / act wisely in his deeds / and will act quickly / he is mischievous /

---

[139] FSC p47 Hydra ... influence: According to Ptolemy the bright Stars are like Saturn and Venus. It is said to give an emotional and passionate nature, threatened by great troubles, and to cause some interest in shipping.

[140] Prokyon or Anticanis are other names for Canis Minor. SH p55, α – Procyon, the name P. comes from the earliest Greek records and means "before the dog", which suggests that the star was seen ... as announcing the rising of Sirius. FSC p191 Procyon ... influence: ... makes its natives petulant, saucy, giddy, weak-natured, timid, unfortunate, proud, easily angered, careless and violent.

[141] FSC p35 Canis Minor ... influence: ... it is said to cause frivolity and either love of dogs or danger of dog-bites.

verbose[142] / he will be more poor than rich / he receives much grace / and does not like to work / and this is why he is more lazy than doing his work.

The other Horse is between Gemini and Cancer

The other horse[143] is a heavenly image / and has xvii. stars / which can hardly be seen / because they are dark / their distribution is as follows / on top of the head are ii. on the neck ii. on each wing ii. on each foot one / on the belly ii under the tail on the knee one / at the bottom of the left wing one.

Who will be conceived or born under this sign[144] / is always rich and not poor / and will receive great honours and worthiness / and will be industrious[145] / and lives tenderly and well / and will be loved by all people / and is honest / and is shamefaced and peaceful.

The Drill [Nebiger][146] is at the end of Sagittarius / and at the end of Capricorn

The Drill[147] is a heavenly image / and has v. stars / their distribution is as follows / on the head of the drill / are ii. on the iron iii. stars.

---

[142] *weitschweiffig*

[143] Known to us as Equuleus, the Foal or Little Horse.

[144] FSC p44 Equuleus ... influence: It gives friendship and sagacity but frivolity and love of pleasure.

[145] *weitschweiffig*

[146] *Nebinger*, as well *nabegêr* or *nebegêr*, from the Middle High German "to drill". According to *Preussisches Wörterbuch*, Berlin 1883, p94 a "Nebinger" is a drill used to drill out the centre of a wheel from which the spokes radiate. Grimm's *Deutsches Wörterbuch* informs us that "at the beginning of spring farmers drill through birch trees with a 'neber' or drill."

[147] This might be the constellation we now know as Sagitta, the Arrow.

Who will be conceived or born under this sign / is always more of a fool than wise / and the wheel of fortune will turn many times for him / he expects[148] more evil than good things / and it befalls him.

The Banner is at the end of Leo and at the beginning of Virgo

The Flag[149] is a heavenly image / and has v. stars / their distribution is as follows / at the front of the iron is one / in the middle of the spear is one / and on the flag are ii. and on each cloth of the flag is one.

Who will be conceived or born under this sign / is of high standing / rich and honest / and will receive great honours and worthiness / he will be loved and honoured / he will take the poverty off people / and is battlesome and warmongering / and overcomes his enemies.

End of the 36 pictures including their stars.

---

[148] *hoffet*

[149] Possibly known to us as Vela.

Part Two

PLANETS

Of the Seven Planets

Of the Order / Manners and Properties of the Planets

The order of the Planets is / first at the bottom after the element of fire is the Moon / above the Moon is Mercury / above Mercury is Venus / above Venus is [the] Sun / above [the] Sun is Mars / above Mars is Jupiter / above Jupiter is Saturn.

Saturn

Old / cold and unclean / hatred and envy too / they are my children / which are born under me.

The first Planet is Saturn / he completes his motion through the zodiac in xxx. years / When Saturn is in his houses / which is in Aquarius and Capricorn / then there is evil in the world / and worst things happen when he is in the first house / it causes high waters and rivers are overflowing / and hatred amongst people. Who is born under Saturn / has little hair on his head and on the cheeks / and is dark under the eyes / and is of brown colour / and likes to look to the ground when he is walking / and has a thin body and small eyes / and has dry skin / and is angry / poisonous / harmful / and rude[150] / and is to do hard labour / like digging / excavating[151] and breaking stones / building houses and funnelling water / and is talking differently with his mouth than he means in his heart. When Saturn rules his houses in his hour be it day or night / who is born then will

---

[150] *uppig*, "impertinent" or "rude"

[151] *telben*, from Middle High German *tëlben*, "to dig".

be harmful / and if somebody is leaving / or travelling he will be lost and never found again / and who is sleeping with women will be harmed / and if something is lost / it will not be found again.

Jupiter

Virtuous and of good manners I am / all who are mine do know / My children can read and write well / they know many arts.

The other Planet is called Jupiter / and he completes his motion through the zodiac in twelve years / When Jupiter is in his house or dwelling / which is Pisces / and a child will be conceived in the next month / so he gives him the mind and the limbs / He bestows to those who are born under him / simple and fine arts / like reading and writing / and exchanging gold / and to handle lovely cloth / of red and white colour / or rose coloured / and has a rather equal measure in stature and length / and has good virtues / and is faithful / and has the front teeth wider and longer than the others / and has long hair and beard / much hair / and is compassionate too.

In Jupiter's hour / if it is in the evening or nocturnal or diurnal / it is good to ask for a duty / and it is good to talk to powerful people / like kings and great masters / and leading animals in bridles[152] / it is beneficial for those who are born in a Jupiter hour / they live long / who is leaving the country / will soon return home with his companions / who has intercourse will succeed / and what has been lost will be found again.

Mars

Looting / burning and killing / Evil deeds are what I do.[153] I am ready for quarrel and discord / as my clothes show. My children are full of hate / they do not know why or how.

---

[152] *gezeugen leiten*

[153] *Ubel thun das ist mein orden*

Mars is the third Planet / and is a star / warm and dry / and is therefore detrimental / and in two years he is travelling completely through the zodiac / and is placed between Jupiter and Venus / they are beneficial stars / and because Mars is [placed] between the two beneficial Planets Venus and Jupiter / therefore he will not do too much harm / If there is a war / Mars is responsible / because he brings heat and dryness / from this results audacity / because the ones who are warm and dry are audacious. When Mars is in his houses which are Aries and Scorpio / he causes laboriousness / war / quarrel / and misfortune in the world / except if would be that his malignity was lessened through a beneficial Planet's aspect / [his] malice is impaired through a beneficial aspect / and its opposite[154] / and his colour is red.

Those who are born under Mars / are brown / red / and mixed / like the ones who are exposed to the Sun / and are a bit scorched / and have red grains under their eyes and [on their] face / and have a small beard / and are abrupt / and are cooks and smiths / and grim shedders of blood / and are cruel and predatory. At a Mars hour it is beneficial to gather the people / who is born will be a pernicious person / who is leaving will be unable to return soon / or will be lost / who has intercourse will be harmed / if something is lost it will not be found again.

Sun

I am concerned with sovereignty / because I am the king of the stars / I proclaim to you at this time / that my radiance outshines all Planets / My rise causes the light of the day / my setting reveals the stars.

[The] Sun is the fourth Planet / and is called Sol / because she alone is shining for all the other stars / or is solely shining for everything that exists on earth / [her] form and shape is of a fiery nature / and is spherical / and is eight times as big as the earth / and gives light to all stars / from dawn until dusk / and is clothed with the envelope of the firmament / but she is

---

[154] *herwiderumb*

shining through the whole of the zodiac / and completes her journey in ccclxv. days / she divides[155] her circle into xxviii. years[156] / and as the Sun is above the Earth all day / so she shines below the Earth all night / When she moves through the north[157] / so she gives us long days and gives us summer / but when she moves through the south[158] she gives us short days and winter.

When the Sun is in her house / which is in Leo / her heat is strongly enraged[159] / these are the dog days. Those who are born under the Sun / they are diligent and have big eyes / and a pale[160] face / large and beautiful / mixed with yellow colour / because the appearance of the Sun is yellow / and she is partially red. Those who are born under the Sun / they are yellow and covered[161] with red / and are beautiful and like to serve God / and are living with great masters / and are dealing with gold / and eventually will become princes and great masters / and live long as well.

Venus

My appearance is pleasant[162] / I quench hatred and envy / My children are prone to courtly love / And are singing with joy.

---

[155] *gradiren*

[156] This seems to refer to the 28 year solar cycle of the Julian calendar.

[157] *Aquilonem,* from the Latin *aquilo, aquilonis,* "north wind", "north".

[158] *Austrum,* from the Latin *austri, australis,* "south wind", "southern".

[159] *erzürnet*

[160] *weisses*

[161] *gedecket*

[162] *frewelich* can have a double meaning because of Middle High German *vrouwe-lich* for "female" or "feminine", but as well Middle High German **vrōuwe* for "pleasure".

Venus is the fifth Planet / and is the evening star / and is the red sky in the morning[163] / and is the head of the son of the light bearer / and is nocturnal and is spherical and fiery / and is shining into the world like Mercury / she is crossing the signs in three hundred and xcviii.[164] days.

When Venus is in her first house Taurus / she quenches hatred / and strengthens love / and has many colours and white / and makes pretty eyes / her children are sweet / mild / and artistic / singers and skippers / and embellish[165] themselves with stringed music / and they like to become masters of stringed music / and love to own nice clothes.

At the Venus hour / be it that it is diurnal or nocturnal / it is good to look for a bride / to send a child to school / this is of use / who is born will live long / who is leaving or travelling will return soon / intercourse will be well / if something is lost it will be found again.

Mercury

Fiery is my nature / and it is characterising my appearance. My children are crafty[166] and subtle / what they do is amusing to them.

Mercury is the sixth Planet / and is spherically shaped / and has a fiery nature / and is as big as the Moon / and still a bit bigger than the Moon / and takes its light and brightness / which he has from the Sun / and crosses the zodiac / through the xii. signs in cccxxxix. days.

Those born under Mercury / have many colours on them / because they are now white / later black / and have a high noble forehead / and a long nose

---

[163] Probably morning star.

[164] this would make 398 days, whereas 687 is the correct number.

[165] *zieren*

[166] *pretty*

/ and a pretty face / and long and subtle cheeks[167] / and are mediocre / and still a bit plumpish[168] / and like to learn to read and write / and what they begin they will finish soon.

On [a] Mercury day or in his hour / be it nocturnal or diurnal / it is good to begin / to send a child to school / and to exhibit something concerning a deed or a matter to a querent[169] or an advocate[170] / that is very good. The ones born here are lively / one who leaves / will return soon / and intercourse is good / and if something is lost / it will be found quickly.

Moon

My body / adopts the nature of all Planets. In the knowledge that my children / are not subservient to anybody.

Luna the Moon is the seventh Planet / the last one from the top he[171] is the seventh / but counted from the ground he is the first Planet and the smallest[172] star / and is not larger than any other of the six stars or Planets[173] / because the Moon will be turned[174] closest to the earth in the first circle / or reversed / and its shape is spherical and not fiery / but he is mixed with

---

[167] *lefftzen*

[168] *feisztlecht*, "stout" or "plumpish".

[169] *kläger*

[170] *fürsprech*

[171] Note that in modern day German the Moon is always male.

[172] *minst*, from Middle High German *minnest, minst*, "smallest" or "least"

[173] *sternen der Planeten*; reading ...*the* (...*stars or Planets*) instead of ...*of* (...*stars of Planets*)

[174] *gewendet*

water and does not have his own light / because he is lit[175] by the Sun as if through a mirror / and this is why the Moon is called Luna / or Lucina / because he takes the light. About the shadows or clouds / visible in the Moon / this is because of the watery nature and would he not be mixed with water the Sun would ignite and scorch the soil because of her closeness / and the earth would be empty and barren / and her ball or sphere is much larger / although we on earth might think / that the balls or spheres of the Sun and the Moon are equal in size / or we think [she would] be bigger / because she is close[r] to the earth / than we think / which is when she rises / and this is why the Moon is shining sideways[176] / because at this moment the Sun is directing her beams towards him[177] / and on the other side it is dark / because the Sun does not shine there / or because he is opposed to the Sun / and if he is furthest away from the Sun he is completely shining[178] / he is neither waxing nor waning / but the reflection of the earth / and the light which is taken from the Sun / can be seen on the firmament each day / that he is turning from rising until setting / and is moving across his circle in xix. years / when the quarter Moon is reddening / he creates winds / when there are black specks in the smoke of the little horns[179] / it means rain at the beginning of the month / but if it is in the middle of the Full Moon / this means it is a bright and pure time.

The Moon is receiver of all fate[180] / because he changes his nature as he pleases / and is an informer of all Planets / and is taking [on] their nature /

---

[175] *entzündt*

[176] Waxing or waning Moon

[177] *anscheinet*

[178] Full Moon

[179] *hörnlein* … German for a "little horn of an animal", but in Anglo-Saxon this could be the horns (pointed extremities) of the Moon in first and last quarters. (I am indebted to Sue Ward who pointed this out to me.)

[180] *zunemer aller schickung.*

because he is visiting all signs and Planets every month / and takes from each individually / and is pouring his beams onto the earth / and we should therefore only look at the Moon in his effect. In the seventh month the Moon is giving a child its lungs / and is dividing its limbs according to its phases[181] / and the child that will be born will be lively / because all Planets will have worked their power on it. If it is the case that it will be born in the eighth month / it will not stay alive. Then it is the case that Jupiter is ruling in him[182] / and he harms nobody / and the ones born under the Moon / he does not make them subservient / and they always want to travel / and they are messengers too / to lie and to carry messages[183] / and legends / and are concerned with serving other people and have one eye bigger than the other / and are rarely different / than [being] cross-eyed or [having] the stone in the eye / or are blind in one eye / or it is unhealthy in another way / and the ones born under the Moon are buying and selling oil[184] and figs / and such things / When the Moon is in a tropical sign[185] / all things are changing [.] Marriage and work / and hate and enmity / and unsteadiness and unstable building[s][186] and to create basement[s] / but it is not of use to begin with the building of castles and places / who will get ill will not stay unhealed[187] for long / and wars will not [last] long too / buying and selling is not of use / because the items one should sell / do not stay with the merchants for long / because they will be taken from them with perfidy and pain and by force / those who will be given an office /

---

[181] meaning is unclear

[182] meaning is unclear

[183] *merlin zutragen*

[184] *oley*

[185] *tropico signo*

[186] this could as well refer to temporary buildings.

[187] *missehelung*

will not benefit from it / and whichever good things will befall one will not last for long / and if somebody promises something to somebody / he will not keep it / but will he give it to him / it will not last long / who is ill will not recover soon / and will get ill again / and if it would be that one would have escaped from prison / if he would escape / he would be captured again / but if one would be captured in time once again / he would be free soon / and if somebody would lose something he would find it again.

In the hour of the Moon if he is nocturnal or diurnal / it is good to put manure on the fields / and it is useful to catch water in cisterns / and the ones to be born will be lively / and who is leaving will return soon / and it is good to have intercourse / and if something gets lost / it will quickly be found again.

Of the Complexion of the Twelve Signs and the Planets

To learn about the fate of the air[188] which can be known from the different movements of the stars / it is necessary to find out / what the signs are capable of / what the Planets are called / and what is the way and virtue of the circle / which is surrounding us by day and night.

There are xii. signs which are differentiated by nature and virtue of the four elements / as well as there are three signs Aries / Leo / and Sagittarius / which are of fiery nature hot and dry. Gemini / Libra / and Aquarius are of airy nature / warm and moist. The seven Planets are of similar nature / Saturn is cold to the highest degree / and is dry / and is therefore hostile against nature / Jupiter is moderate / warm and moist / and therefore he is friendly towards nature / he is more hot than moist / Mars is harshly hot and dry choleric / He is not a friend of life / his heat is more than his moisture or dryness / The Sun is quite warm and dry / and is in the middle between the four elements / Venus is quite warm[189] and very moist / and is

---

[188] Meaning unclear to me.

[189] The nature of Venus is described to be either hot and moist or cold and moist by various authors. William Lilly writes in *Christian Astrology* that

ruling over lovers[190] / Mercury is leaning equally / towards the Planets and signs next to him / but he is said to be cold and dry / the Moon is quite warm and very moist / he is called a well of moistness / as the Sun is called a well of heat / although they are moderately hot in the aforementioned signs /

Different kinds of strengths are attributed to the Planets / which are called / might[191] and power[192] / and dignities or testimonies of the Planets / as there are the domiciles / exaltation or triplicity / or his term[193] the aspect or face[194] / the domicile has the strength or might of ii.[195] / exaltation four / triplicity has iii. the term ii. the face i. and as well has the domicile the strength of five faces[196] on him / as well in the others /

The domicile can be compared to a man / who is in his own house or works with his own power / exaltation equals a man who is in his empire and rules / the triplicity is equal to a man who is in his honour / and with the ones who are helping him / and the term is equal to a man who is amongst

---

Venus would be both, sanguine and phlegmatic (CA p73). This may lead us to the conclusion that Venus, when being seen as the lesser benefic, is of hot and moist nature (sanguine) but, on the other hand, being feminine, she is of cold and moist nature (phlegmatic) too.

[190] *buler*, from Middle High German *buole*

[191] *vermögenheit*

[192] *mächtigkeit*

[193] *ende*

[194] *aspect oder anblick*

[195] This is unclear; note that in the same paragraph the domicile ruler is given 5 points.

[196] *aspecte*

his friends and his race / face or aspect is compared to a man in his mastery / A good aspect is like a mighty army with its king / a bad aspect is like an army against him /

These are the exaltations of the Planets / Sun is exalted in Aries / the Moon in Taurus / Saturn in Libra / Jupiter in Cancer / Mars in Capricorn / Venus in Pisces / Mercury in Virgo / Acknowledge now how the Sun is exalted / according to her strength in Aries / so it is in the following signs / a domicile of a Planet is the sign wherein it was created / at the beginning of the world / and therefore Leo is the domicile of the Sun / Cancer of the Moon / Virgo [of] Mercury / Libra [of] Venus / Aries [of] Mars / Sagittarius [of] Jupiter / Capricorn [of] Saturn's domicile /

Now learn that five Planets receive some power / in the five remaining signs / like Saturn in Aquarius / Jupiter in Pisces / Mars in Scorpio / Venus in Taurus / Mercury in Gemini / the first [ones] are called their special houses / but the five others are called applied domicile[s][197] /

Now it is called triplicity of a Planet / when he is in a sign which is of such nature as is the sign it was created in / for example if the Sun is in Aries or Sagittarius / because these two signs are warm and dry / as well as Leo wherein the Sun has been created / and when the Moon is in Scorpio or in Pisces / which are cold and moist / as well as Cancer wherein the Moon was created / and so it is as well with the others / which is each Planet's term / and they are unequal / but the terms of the Egyptians / are the most acceptable[198] / and they are these / Jupiter has the first six degrees of Aries / Venus the six following ones and so on[199] like [in] the table which has been made about it[200] /

---

[197] *zufallende wohnung*

[198] *fürnemste*

[199] *fürbas*

[200] The missing table can be found in the introduction.

The faces of the signs are differentiated like thus / each sign is split into iii. equal parts / and each part has x. degrees / they are called faces[201] / these faces are also called decanates[202] / [they] begin in the first degree of Aries / and therefore is the first face[203] from the first degree of Aries to the tenth the term of Mars / from the tenth degree to the twentieth degree it is the Sun's / because she is after Mars in the order of the Planets / the third term is Venus' / from xx. degrees until the end of Aries / and so forth one after the other of the others / the formerly stated attributes are taken from the signs /

There are other strengths a Planet can receive from the others / a Planet will be strengthened and weakened through a bad aspect / and [there] are five aspects / opposition[204] / square trine sextile / opposition happens if a Planet is in one sign / opposite the other / and this aspect is the worst / mainly if the Planets are of unequal nature / and the signs as well / for example if Venus [is] in Aries / and Saturn is in Libra / because it is a sign opposed to the other / and one Planet is opposed to the other / and everything is contradicted / in the nature of the signs and Planets / A trine aspect is / when two are in an equal sign / and have between them a quarter of the firmament / this aspect is the best of all / because there is no contradiction in the nature of the signs / and if it is / that the Planets are in harmony with the signs / like Jupiter and Venus / there is no contradiction / a square aspect is / when there are three whole signs between the Planets / like the Sun is in Aries / and Saturn in Cancer / and a square aspect / between the aforementioned Planets [takes up] a quarter of the circle of the firmament / this aspect is bad / the sextile aspect is if there are two whole signs between two other Planets / this is the sixth part of the circle of the

---

[201] *aspectus*

[202] *zehender*

[203] *anblick*

[204] *oppositz / Gegenschein*

xii. signs / and is mediocre in harmony / the signs in a willing conjunction of the Planets / is generally if two Planets are in one sign and one degree / stargazers are calling this the strongest aspect / but we think that ♉ is three times stronger[205] / there are other debilities which the Planets may receive because they are different in their short ascension / which is called epicycle[206] / As well there are rising / setting / direct movement / standstill / retrogradation / and detriment / Rise of a Planet means that it moves out of the sunbeams[207] / and visibly appears in the world [so] that it is not interfered[208] by the sunbeams[209] / Setting is an entrance into the sunbeams / Direct movement or flight[210] / is called if a Planet is moving visibly[211] against the firmament behind it / if it is moving[212] against the firmament with fast movement[213] / [It] is called standing still if it is staying in a minute for long / their strength is changing according to the closer or further distance from the medium coeli[214] / if they are close up their

---

[205] The meaning of this sentence is unclear.

[206] *Epicicclus*

[207] *glast*

[208] *Irret, irren,* according to the *Pfälzische Wörterbuch: behindern, stören,* "to obstruct" or "to interfere".

[209] A Planet is said to be "under the Sun's beams" when it is between 17.5° and 8° from the Sun.

[210] *Flecht*, probably from *Flucht*, Old High German *fluht*, "to escape", related to the English word "flight".

[211] *empfintlich*

[212] *genger*

[213] *zückender bewegung*, from Middle High German *zücken* or *zucken*, "a fast movement".

[214] *... scheitel höhe unser häupter*

influence is stronger / if they are further away from it / the effect is proportionally weaker / There is as well a difference between the three upper Planets / and on the iii. lower ones how they are different in their orbits[215] / Each Planet has more power in the upper part of his orbit / and less amongst the others to work against these lowly things / and this is because of their speed of the daily motion[216] / if it is in the large arc or in the further distance / it is moved faster / as if it is in the larger arc or in the closer distance / which is in the lower part of his orbit / these are the applying testimonies of the Planets in their circles / which are necessary to recognize these things.

A few Spheres are following after this

Of the Dignities of Planets

There are five particular dignities / which the Planets have in the twelve signs / that is Domus / Exaltatio / Triplicitas / Terminus / and Aspectus / Domus is the house / Exaltatio is the exaltation / Triplicitas is triplicity or an equality / this is because the nature of the Planet and the nature of the sign are equal / Term [or] a target[217] / Facies a face. When a Planet is in its house / it has a strength of five / and therein it is powerful and mighty / like a great master who is in his house or castle / But if a Planet is in exaltation / it has four strengths / and is a great master who is in his majesty and sovereignty / But when a Planet is in triplicity / it has three strengths / and therein he is like a master who is amongst his helpers / When a Planet is in its term / it has two strengths / and is like a master who is amongst his kin / and amongst his native friends / But when a Planet is in its face / it has one strength / and is like a master / who is amongst good friends.

---

[215] *hintraeger*

[216] *Umkreisung*, literally "circumambulation".

[217] *zil*

Of the Joy of Planets

Apart from these particular five dignities / each Planet has another dignity / which is called its joy / and is as follows.

Saturn has its joy in Aquarius / because it is a masculine sign / Jupiter has its joy in Sagittarius / Mars in Scorpio / the Sun in Leo / Venus in Taurus / Mercury in Virgo / and the Moon in Cancer. There is another Planetary joy on the heavenly circle / and is as follows / Mercury has its joy in the descendant / The Moon in the third house / Venus in the fifth house / Mars in the sixth house / The Sun in the ninth house / Jupiter in the eleventh house / Saturn in the twelfth house.

Of the Fall of Planets

Now learn / Saturn is in its fall in Aries / Jupiter in Capricorn / Mars in Cancer / Sun in Libra / Venus in Virgo / Mercury in Pisces / Moon in Scorpio. Now it should be known / if a Planet is in its dignity / or in a good place / it is not unchaste / although it is evil otherwise / but if it is in a place which is against it / it shows its malice and its bad habits.

Amongst the twelve signs are two which are most dignified / they are Leo and Cancer / and their Planets / which are the Sun / and the Moon [are] the most dignified amongst all Planets. The Sun acts more in the day than during the night / and the Moon more during the night than at daytime / as we have written before / but the Moon has still more power during the day / than the Sun during the night / The Sun signifies[218] the air / and the Moon earth and water.

Masculine and Feminine Planets and Signs

The Planets have particular effects / according to masculinity or femininity / and this shall be understood in the way / that each sign is either masculine or feminine / masculinity is understood to be hot and dry / and femininity is understood to be cold and moist / all warm signs / are

---

[218] *bezeichnen*

masculine / and all that are cold are feminine / The same has to be understood with the Planets / Saturn / Jupiter and the Sun are masculine / and Venus and the Moon are feminine. Mars is feminine / although he is hot / and Mercury is masculine in masculine signs / and feminine in feminine signs / The night is feminine / the day is masculine / and one should know / that masculine Planets have a stronger effect during the day than during the night / so if a masculine Planet is in a masculine sign during daytime / or a feminine Planet in a feminine sign during night time / so it is placed well and is simply doing its work / but if a masculine Planet is in a feminine sign during the night / or a feminine Planet in a masculine sign during the day / it is in a debilitated state[219] and is not doing anything good.

The Characteristics of the Planets

Now learn about the Planets / Saturn is vastly cold and dry / and therefore if he has no resistance / he is an enemy of nature. Jupiter is warm and moist in the right order / and therefore he is a friend of nature / but in him the heat is stronger / than the moisture. Mars is vastly hot and dry / and therefore he is an enemy of nature / and is more hot than dry. The Sun is warm and dry in natural order / and the Sun is well mannered[220] towards all natures. Mercury is cold and dry himself / but he takes on the nature of each of the Planets he is with. The Moon is moderately cold and excessively moist. Dragon's head is warm and dry / Dragon's tail is cold and moist.

Of [the] Aspect or Sight of the Planets

The views or the aspects of signs and Planets / are called as follows / conjunctio / oppositio / quartus aspectus dexter / quartus aspectus sinister / trinus aspectus dexter / trinus aspectus sinister / sextilis aspectus dexter / and sextilis aspectus sinister.

---

[219] *kränklich*

[220] *geordenet*

An aspect is the sight the signs have of each other / or the Planets.

Conjunction is / if a Planet is with another one in one sign / and in the same degree / as if Saturn and Jupiter were together in the sixth degree of Aries.

Opposition is if a Planet is away from another one in the seventh sign / and still in the same degree / as if one Planet would be in the sixth degree of Aries / and the other one would be in the sixth degree of Libra.

Square aspect / is out of one sign over two signs / as if a Planet would be in the sixth degree of Aries / and the other in the sixth degree of Cancer / they look at each other in ninety degrees.[221]

Trine aspect / is if a Planet looks at another one in the v. sign / as if a Planet would be in the sixth degree of Aries / and the other one would be in the sixth degree of Leo.

Sextile aspect is as if a Planet looks at another one in the third sign / as if a Planet would be in the sixth degree of Aries / and the other one would be in the sixth degree of Gemini.

There are more Planetary aspects / like in the next sign / and in the sixth sign / and in the eighth sign / and in the twelfth sign / but these are not called aspects by the masters / because they are ill / and imbalanced in their harmony[222] / and are more harmful than good.

Of [the] Significance of Aspects

Square aspect / is strong and signifies hidden enmity / opposition is still stronger and signifies open enmity. Conjunction causes change of things / sextile aspect / signifies friendship / trine aspect / signifies complete

---

[221] *quarto gradu*

[222] *getön*, from the Latin "tonus", Middle High German loanword for "melodious sound".

friendship / and this because / the signs in the trine aspect are of the same nature.

Of Strength and Weakness of the Planets

As the Planets have strength in some signs / they are weak and ill in some signs too / If a Planet is in the house of his enemy / it is not well / and is unlucky / as well if a Planet is in Casuso / that is in its fall / it is not well placed.

Of the Beginning of the Year / how one has to take heed / wherein Planets and Signs the Sun or the Moon will enter / and to judge accordingly

Revolution of the year[223] / this is the beginning of the year / when the Sun has moved through the twelve signs / and returns in the first minute of Aries / and this is called the beginning of the year / or *revolutio anni* / which is / when the Sun moves into Aries / and according to that time one notes how the year will be / if the Sun is in a bad aspect with Saturn or Mars at the time / it indicates a contamination of the air / But if the Moon is in a bad place / or a bad aspect with Saturn or Mars / it indicates a contamination of the earth or water. The bad or unlucky Planets are Saturn and Mars / Saturn with cold / Mars with heat / and if Mercury is their helper / it is very bad too.

Of the Lord of the Year

Who wants to know the movements of time / has to look at the Lord of the year[224] first / because all other Planets are orientated according to it all year / Note when the Sun rises in the first minute of Aries / one has to look for the Lord of the year / and / if a Planet is then in the ascendant / that is in the rising sign / it is Lord of the year / and you are not allowed to look for

---

[223] *Revolutio anni*

[224] *Dominum anni*

another / but if there is none in the ascendant you have to look for it in the other angles / and if you find one in the middle of heaven / it is Lord of the year / or in the west[225] or the north[226] / but if there is none in the iiii. angles / so look which Planet has most power and dignity in the ascendant / Like triplicity ruler[227] / exaltation[228] / term[229] / and face[230] / and this one is Lord of the year /

Note as well if the sign on the ascendant[231] at the same time is a fixed sign / being Aries[232] / Leo / Scorpio / and Aquarius / then the Planet is Lord of the year for the whole year / but if it is a common sign / like Gemini / Virgo / Sagittarius and Pisces / then the Planet looked for will be Lord of the year for not more than half a year / it is until the Sun moves into Libra / and then another one has to be found / But if the sign on the ascendant[233] / at the ingress of the Sun / into Aries is a moveable sign like Aries / Cancer / Libra and Capricorn / one has to find another one at each quarter of the year. This is / when the Sun moves into Cancer / and when she moves into Capricorn. Some of the masters say / when the Sun moves into Aries / one has to look what the ascendant would be / and which Planet has most power and dignity in the ascendant / wherever in the heavens it might be /

---

[225] *nidergang*

[226] *Mittnacht*

[227] *Domus Triplicitatem,* reading Dominus Triplicitatem instead.

[228] *exaltationem*

[229] *terminum*

[230] *faciem*

[231] *signum ascendens*

[232] *Wider,* this is obviously an error as the fourth fixed sign is Taurus.

[233] *signum ascendens*

it would still be Lord of the year / but the first rule is more approved and comes closer to the truth.

And it is the opinion of Ptolemy and Hali and Messahalla and Albumasar and the others of the highest masters of the study of celestial bodies[234] / that one should observe the conjunction or opposition / of the Sun and Moon / which is closest amongst the ii. before the ingress of the Sun into the first minute of Aries and has to look what the ascendant might be / at the time it becomes new / or opposed / and which Planet would be Lord of the ascendant[235] / it is ruler of the sign / and its nature shall be combined with the nature of the Planet which is Lord of the year[236] / and if they are of the same nature / then the significance is much greater and stronger / but if one is hot and the other cold / or one dry and the other one wet / one is causing the other to be of average effect. One has to look as well where the iiii. angles are positioned / this is / east[237] / south[238] / west[239] / north[240] / if good or bad Planets are therein / and how the Planets which are the Lords of the signs are placed / if they have something in common with the good or the bad / As well one should look at the conjunction or opposition before the ingress of the Sun in Cancer / in Libra / in Capricorn / and before the ingress of the Sun in every sign.

---

[234] *Astronomia,* from Middle High German *Astronomîe* which is *Sterndeutung* or "stargazing".

[235] *dominus ascendentis*

[236] *dominus anni*

[237] *Aufgang* (Ascendant)

[238] *Mittag* (10th house)

[239] *Nidergang* (7th house)

[240] *Mittnacht* (4th house)

Of the Significance of the Lords and Houses

Learn here now / as the masters write / if a bad Planet is in the ascendant at the time of the Sun's ingress into Aries / it will be a bad year / but if a good Planet is therein it will be a good year / If a bad Planet is in the west[241] / there is a year of war / But if a good Planet is therein / then it is peace.

The eighth sign from the ascendant describes death / If there is a bad Planet therein at the given time / death will occur / But if a good Planet is therein / death will not occur / when somebody dies / it moves over the sign of the viii. house / and the sign of the bad Planet [and] the constellation of the stars / which were standing in the viii. house.

The sixth sign or the sixth house from the ascendant describes sickness and illness not causing death / depending on the bad or good Planet[s] therein.

The tenth sign describes the whole country / and if a bad Planet is therein / the country or empire will be dry[242] / if it is Saturn hunger and drought will follow / or what else comes from frost or drought / but if it is Mars / war and a fire in the country will follow / but if a good Planet is there and not a bad one / it will go well. As the tenth house medium coeli / describes the country or the empire / the Planet belonging to this sign describes / the ruler of the country or empire / If the Planet is in a bad place / the ruler will be ailing / but if he is in a good place or with a good Planet / he will be well.

In the fourth house which is in the north[243] / one can see how the weather will be / if there are moist Planets therein / it indicates rain / are dry Planets therein / it indicates dryness / if Mercury is therein / it indicates wind.

---

[241] *Occident*

[242] *gewinnt ... einen truck.*

[243] *Mitnacht*

Take note now / that the ascendant is not the same in every country / because the signs do not rise in the same way in every country / and therefore the Lord of the year is not the same in every country / and it is because of the breadth and the width / or the plateaus of a country[244] / or because of the tightness and the mountains of a country. It is not the same in all climates too for the same reason / but when the Sun moves into Aries / or into Libra / then day and night are equal in all the world / and this is why the Lord of the year is looked for more at this time than any other time. After you have found the Lord of the year / so observe / [if] Saturn is Lord of the year / it will be very cold / and fog and hailstones will appear / and the people will be [suffering from] rheumatism[245] and gloomy / and will easily catch a cough / and a cold / and gripes[246] / and a tightness around the chest / which is the source of whooping.[247] He also creates hate and envy / and disagreement[248] / and [a] time of drought / the Jews will be well / what is precious / will be rejected / and coarse things will become valuable / and the peasants will be hateful and envious towards their masters / and towards the mighty ones.

If Jupiter is Lord of the year / the weather will be good / and [it will be a] fertile time / and intestinal diseases[249] will be seen amongst people / and

---

[244] *Schlechte*, according to the Rheinische Wörterbuch a "plateau" or "mountainous region".

[245] Flüssig, from Old High German *fluzîc*, "liquid" but also used by Paracelsus for "rheumaticus", or "cattharho fluens".

[246] *krimen*, from Middle High German *krimmen*, later *Grimmen*, "gripes", "colic pains".

[247] *keichen, keuchen* from Middle High German *kîchen*, "to whoop".

[248] *mißhelung* probably the opposite of *hellung*, which is, according to Elsässisches Wörterbuch, "agreement" or "consent".

[249] *darmgesicht*

there will be sanctity amongst people / and priests and clergy are offered[250] discipline[251] and honour / heathens and Jews will be oppressed[252] and despised and the Christians supported / and all nobility will be elevated and honoured.

If Mars is Lord of the year / much heat will be in its time / which is in Summer / and will be moderate at other times / and people will have pains in their heads / and the blood will be contaminated / and the bile will increase / and hot diseases will occur / like the tertian fever[253] / and bumps[254] / it will be war / stabbing / beating / murder / and the nobility will be honoured / and common people[255] will be scorned / and [there] will be great hatred amongst chaplains.

If the Sun is Lord of the year / the weather will be clear / and crops of the earth will be good / and the people will be chaste / and war will end / but people will have diseases of the liver / it will be a fruitful year / nobility and priests will be honoured / and the deceived people will be humiliated.

If Venus is Lord of the year / it will be a wet year / and there will be much fruit / and weeds will grow amidst it / and people will be unchaste / and [it] will be a wild time with dancing and courting / and there will be

---

[250] *beutten*

[251] *zucht*

[252] *getruckt*

[253] *drittaglich frörer* or "febris tertiana".

[254] *beulen*, "bumps", probably synonymous with the bubonic plague.

[255] *unadel*

unanimity amongst the clergy / and what is noble and good will be dishonourable[256] / and what is graceful and pretty / will be valued.

If Mercury is Lord of the year / the weather will be unsettled / now warm [and] now cold / now dry [and] now wet / and makes the most wind / and rain / and there will be much betrayal / and there will be much enmity[257] / deceit and evil sins will be conceived / but if he is well positioned / and with good Planets / then he is good / Scribes / priests and clergy / advocates / they will be proud and cocky / and what is moderate / will be of value.

If the Moon is Lord of the year / there will be lots of heavy rain / and many illnesses will appear / and particularly bumps[258] / and continuous fever[259] / and the year will not be overly fruitful / and people will become unsteady in their ways and moods / and the things for one's basic needs like food and drink / will easily rot and deteriorate / It has to be understood that these things are not happening all over the world / it should be understood in the way / that it happens in the country / which the sign belongs to / in which the Planet is Lord of the year / or Lord of the quarter.

Note as well / if there is a Planet with it / hindering it / and is working against [the] Lord of the year's influence / nothing will come of it / It should be noted too / that the heaven and all stars / have their influence and nature from God / who is a creator of all beings / and he has reserved it for himself / to cause supernatural effects / and therefore what is written here / is written as a possibility / and not as a certainty / because the masters envisioned it / when a star was in a certain position / as they wrote

---

[256] *unachtbar*, from Middle High German *unachtbære*, opposite of *achtbar*, "honourable".

[257] *auffsetz*, from *aufsatz*, meaning "enmity" or "stalking".

[258] *die beule*, "the bump", probably synonymous for bubonic plague.

[259] *alletäglich frörer*

/ the effects will always follow / as it is written down / but we have to give the honour to God / that he may turn cold [into] hot / and hot [into] cold / and may turn dry [into] wet / and wet [into] dry / and turn bad into good / so it all pleases his divine order / whose name be blessed and praised / amen.

Of Dignity and Elevation of one Planet Above the Other / and its meaning

Of Venus' Elevation

If Venus is elevated above Mercury / one is winning over another[260] / and if Venus is exalted above the Moon / people are happy / and the music is sweet / if Venus is elevated above Mars / women are fertile / and people will have stomach aches due to the abundance of food and drink / if Venus is elevated above the Sun / the people are mild and spend much / if Venus is elevated above Jupiter / it indicates [a] good time / if Venus is elevated above Saturn / it brings cramps / the gripes[261] and periodic rheumatism.[262]

Of Jupiter

If Jupiter is elevated above the Moon / nobility will come forward / and grow in virtue and in honour / if Jupiter is elevated above Mercury / civil servants will be happy / their masters will find them useful / and will praise and honour them / if Jupiter is elevated above Mars / it brings illness and disease / if Jupiter is elevated above Saturn / it indicates sadness / pains and weeps / if Jupiter is elevated above the Dragon's Tail / it indicates the destruction of several buildings / If Jupiter is elevated above a comet / nobility will not do well.

---

[260] ... *so ligt einer dem anderen ob;* from Old High German *obba ligan,* "on top of" or "superior"

[261] *krimmen*

[262] *gesücht*

Of Mars

If Mars is elevated above Mercury / it indicates war / quarrel / beating and stabbing / if Mars is elevated above the Moon / it indicates earthquakes / if Mars is elevated above Jupiter / noblemen will pick up their weapons / and are thinking of how one will kill the other / if Mars is elevated above Saturn / it does not indicate much evil / and if Mars is elevated above the Dragon's Head / it will bring great heat.

Of the Sun

If the Sun is elevated above the other Planets / it does not indicate much good / apart from above Mercury.

Of the Moon

If the Moon is elevated above Mercury / it indicates / that people will be of good senses and good council / if the Moon is elevated above Venus / it indicates that the noble and the rich / and the women will have an increase in honour and kindness[263] / if the Moon is elevated above Jupiter / it indicates that the king and the great masters will have an increase in honour and in power / if the Moon is elevated above Mars / it indicates burning and bloodshed / if the Moon is elevated above Saturn / it indicates treason / murder / and ill will / if the Moon is elevated above the Dragon's Head / it indicates that the wells will have a low water level / and if the Moon is elevated over the Dragon's Tail / it indicates death amongst people and animals / and if the Moon is elevated over a comet / it indicates destruction of things / and if this happens under the Sun's beams / it indicates most evil and destruction.

Of Mercury

If Mercury is elevated above the Moon / it indicates pleasure / and that the people will do strange things / and if Mercury is elevated above Venus / it

---

[263] *gůt, Güte*, "kindness"

indicates that people will succumb[264] to black magic / and if Mercury is elevated above Jupiter / it indicates that there will be more kings / and noblemen will stay capable[265] and in honour / and if Mercury is elevated above Mars / it indicates that people are fearful / and if Mercury is elevated above Saturn / one will betray the other / and if Mercury is elevated above the Dragon's Head / it indicates that many murders will be heard about / and if Mercury is elevated above the Dragon's Tail / it indicates that people will ridicule themselves / and each other / and if it is elevated above a comet / it indicates that the best and richest will be stabbed.

Of the Elevation of the Dragon's Head

If the Dragon's Head is elevated above the Sun / it indicates damage / and if it is elevated above Venus / it indicates good [things] and betterment of women's duties / and of virgins' / and joy / and if it is elevated above Mercury / it means that people will take it upon themselves[266] to build houses / and strongholds and villages / and towns / but also destruction / and if the Dragon's Head is elevated above the Moon / it indicates damage to transported goods / and if it is elevated above Saturn / it indicates that war will begin / and that people will arm themselves / elevated over a comet / it indicates many violent storms.

Of the Elevation of the Dragon's Tail

If the Dragon's Tail is elevated above the Sun / it indicates much evil and sadness / elevated above a comet / it indicates damage to women's duties.

Of the Elevation of a comet

A comet elevated above Venus / indicates diminishing and declining of the waters / elevated above Mercury / it indicates damage and destruction

---

[264] *unterwinden*, from Old High German *untarwintan*, "to succumb to".

[265] *in vermüglicheit*, from *vermöglich*, "to be capable of".

[266] *unterwinden*

amongst young people / elevated above the Moon / indicates damage and destruction of all things / elevated above Saturn / it indicates great and strong illnesses / elevated above Jupiter / it indicates that noblemen will be stabbed / elevated above Mars / indicates that people will take it upon themselves to be armed / and great confiscations[267] will take place amongst them / elevated above the Dragon's Head / the precious ones and the noblemen will be stabbed / elevated above the Dragon's Tail / makes great loss and damage amongst the trees / elevated above Mercury / indicates that people will be at war with each other with great disloyalty.

Of Saturn's Elevation

Saturn elevated above the Moon / indicates that nefarious customs will befall people / elevated above Jupiter / indicates / that noblemen and the mighty will be stabbed / elevated above Mars / indicates good things and betterment in all things / elevated above the Dragon's Head / indicates noblemen's joy and happiness / elevated above the Dragon's Tail / it indicates good things for the poor and the common people / elevated above Venus / indicates that people will take it upon themselves to do masterly things / in paintings and such like.

These judgements and verdicts we have spoken of / will be determined by the Planets / if one is elevated above the other / or if one is conjunct another / and if one's ray is falling onto another.

Of the Conjunctions of the Planets and their Meaning

If Venus is conjunct Mars during the course of a year / drastic events will take place in Rome and the country / Venus conjunct Jupiter / indicates a great lack of bread and food / Mercury conjunct Saturn indicates an affliction of churches and hallmarks[268] / Mars conjunct Jupiter indicates

---

[267] *niderlegung*

[268] *beizeichen*, "attribute", "hallmark"

kings' deaths from afflictions / and indicates many lizards[269] / Mercury conjunct Mars / bad things will happen / Jupiter conjunct Saturn / indicates the death of the king of the mightiest in the world / Mercury conjunct Moon / indicates affliction and the death of people / If Luna is eclipsing and covering Saturn / the mighty king will die at the declination / the Moon conjunct Venus or conjunct Jupiter / and if Venus casts its ray over the Moon / then there will be many riches and much betterment coming to people / and if the Moon is hiding from Venus / so that he casts no ray / it indicates the death of a king when rising / and if this conjunction is with Jupiter / then it is dreadful to live in the west / if Jupiter and Mars are in one sign / the king will be harmed until it has moved lxxv. days and nights. Venus conjunct Saturn shows great fear in the east / if Mars is at the head of its domicile / or in its centre / it indicates that the kings are stabbing each other / in the part of the world / where Mars is standing / and if it is that Saturn is in the constellation we mentioned before / it indicates great poverty / if Mars is in the centre of Algelihe or in Mulione / these are stars of that name / it indicates poverty and fear / and if Mars is in the centre of Adanandam / it indicates deadliness.

If Jupiter joins Saturn from the iii. or the vi.[270] it indicates that the ones preaching the law / and the ones stipulating the secret things of the kings will be honoured / and if it is / that the aspect is from the iiii.[271] it indicates rebellions against the king / and indicates great changes in the king's duty / and equally for the laws / and if it is that this iiii. aspect is from its x.[272] it indicates much war and dissension[273] / and war amongst the kings / and if

---

[269] *egdessen, egdesse,* from Middle High German *egedëhse,* High German *Eidechse.*

[270] Trine or sextile

[271] Square aspect

[272] A dexter square

[273] *misshelle*

it is that the aspect is from the opposition[274] / it indicates much war amongst the people and amongst the kings / one against the other / and indicates many clouds.

If Mars is conjunct Saturn / then one is disloyal and treacherous to the other / and many miracles will happen / and the king will be hindered in his work / by the people of the region who are against him / and if Mars applies to Saturn from iii. or vi. it indicates work and damage to people's work and in the king's properties and his laws / and if it is that this aspect is from the iiii. it indicates that many thieves and murderers will be disclosed / and if it is that this four is from the x. much anxiety and evil will happen / because of the king / when his [people] are disobedient to him / and if it is that the application[275] is from the opposition / it means that the people are not in agreement amongst each other / and hate each other and bear witness against each other.

Sun conjunct Saturn means that lies and deceits are in people / and if it is and applying [aspect] from the 3rd or sixth the king will be poor / and it is important to him that he will get on with his people / and if its application is from the x. and if it is that it is from its x. house / it indicates that the kings are doing their things in secrecy / and if it is that it is in its x. / it indicates that the king will be fearful and will have much work to do / and if it is that this aspect is an opposition / then it indicates / that the kings are opposed to the clerics / and that they will be separated from the world.

Venus conjunct Saturn indicates that the children being born / will be fearful and sad / and it will be a bad year / and particularly in Egypt / there will be much dissent and war / and the waters will be full of precious

---

[274] *gegenwertigkeit*

[275] *applicatio*

stones / and if this aspect is from the iii.[276] or xi.[277] it indicates damage in pregnant women / because they will have much work to do / and if it is that this application is from the x. and if it is that it is from the x. house / that means / that women will have war and problems[278] with their husbands / and amongst themselves / and if it is that it is / from its x. it indicates that nothing will work out for women / who want things against better knowledge[279] / for kings or their master's wants and will have many accidents / All things influenced by Venus will be spoilt / like scoffers and suchlike / being of the nature of Venus / and if it is that the application is from the opposition / it indicates that the women will have war and much business with their husbands.

Mercury conjunct Saturn indicates that people will take it upon themselves to work black magic / and trickery[280] / and scribes will be hindered / because they will be despised / and if it is that another Planet applies to it / from the iii. or vi. it means that the people who live with the king / will take it upon themselves to read books / and if it is that a Planet applies to it from the iiii. and from its iiii. house / it indicates that the secrecy of black magic and trickery will be hidden / and if it is from its x. house / it indicates that many books will be hidden / and that people will take it upon themselves to practice black magic / and if it is that this application is from the opposition / it indicates that people will be deceitful / and books will be faked.

---

[276] A sinister trine

[277] A dexter trine

[278] *arbeit*

[279] *...wider ihren willen*

[280] *geucherei*, from *gäuchen*, "to do something foolish", but as well *gaukelei*, "trickery" or "magic".

The Moon conjunct Saturn / indicates much work and sadness and damage to people in dungeons and similar [places] / and depravation of the trees / and the animals / and much water / and if it is that [a Planet] applies to it / from the iii. or the vi. indicates false witness and beatings and dungeons / fear and sadness / and therefore cholera breaks out / and there will be much sadness and depravation in many places / and buildings / and the women will give birth to many dead children / and there will be much snow / which will destroy many people / and people like to plant and build / and dig holes and ditches / and if it is that the application is from iiii. and from its iiii. house / people will have many dreams and fears and frightening things of a melancholy nature and similar things / and if it is that it is from its x. dissent and war will happen to the king and the mighty ones / and many will be captured because of the lack of unanimity[281] of the kings / and it creates great fear / And if it is from the application [of the opposition] / it indicates that the people will be sad and will have much work to do.

Mars conjunct Jupiter indicates much war / and many wounds and beatings / and afflictions and death or strength[282] in the part of the world / where the conjunction takes place / Precious animals in different colours will appear in the air / and in the beginning there will be enough to eat / It indicates the death of a king in the same part as well / and if it is that there is an application from the iii. or vi. it indicates hostile actions because of laws / and if it happens from the iiii. it indicates that many will rebel / and terrible people / and murder and such like / and if it is that the application is from the opposition then there will be many marvels amongst people / as well that one will accuse the other of theft / and the king is doing much bad and evil things to his people.

---

[281] *unhelligkeit*

[282] *starckheit,* similar to "strength" and opposed to "weakness"; the word fell out of use in the middle of the 17th century. Its meaning in this context is not entirely clear to me.

The Sun conjunct Jupiter indicates that just people will be lost / and the judges / and there will be damage to the laws / and if there is an application / from the iii. or vi. it indicates that laws and wisdom will appear and will become obvious / and the wise will be honoured / and most of it the laws / and if it is that the application is from the iiii. and from its iiii. [house] it indicates that the judges will judge in a just manner / And if it is from its x. it indicates that law and justice will appear / and will become apparent / and if it is that the application will come from the [opposition] aspect / it will bring much justice and pleasure to the people.

Venus conjunct Jupiter means chastity amongst women / and that they have a good place to do their work / and spices will be valuable and expensive in the places of the parts of the world where this happens / and nourishment will be good and plenty / and the women will be true and chaste to their husbands / and will be rich / and if it is that the application is from the iii. or vi. it indicates that women will like the laws / and stick to them / and provide their husbands with a good place / and if it is that this aspect is from the iiii. or vii.[283] it indicates that the kings' wives will do good work.

Mercury conjunct Jupiter indicates that the people want to know about art / writing and wisdom / laws and secret things / and if it is / that this conjunction is separating from Mars / it indicates afflictions and great heat in the air / and if there is an application from the iii. or vi. it indicates that the people will have many scuffles and brawls / and the law / and if it is that the application is from the iiii. and if it is that it is from their iiii. [house] it indicates many disputes and war will break out amongst those wise in the law / when they are thinking about the laws and the secrecy / and if it is that it is from its x. means that the kings want to know a lot / and are researching / and love books / and women / and if it is / that this application is from the opposition / it indicates that people live amongst each other with suspicion.

---

[283] Trine or opposition

The Moon conjunct Jupiter / indicates that people will take it upon themselves to learn the arts / and to preach the laws / and to build churches / and to explore the laws / and if it is that the application is from the iii. or the vi. it indicates that the laws will be unveiled / wisdom and prophecies / and if it is that this application is from the iiii. and from its iiii. [house] it indicates that people are hiding the laws / and if it is from its x. it indicates that the mighty ones will be elevated and honoured / and churches / and chapels will be built / And if the application is from the opposition / it means unfamiliarity with the laws.

The Sun conjunct Mars indicates much war and dreadful things / in the east / and if the application is from the iii. or [the] vi. / [it] indicates that the kings will be taught justice / and are judging according to the proper laws / and if this application is from the iiii. or its iiii. [house] it indicates that people will be very quiet / because they hide their opinions / and if it is from its x. [it] indicates that the kings will judge unjustly / and there will be fires in the air and in all growing herbs and trees / and if it is that the application is from the opposition / [it] indicates much dreadful war.

Venus conjunct Mars means much unchastity in women / and that the king of Rome dies / and he will suffer much work and poverty / And if it is that there is an application from three or six / it indicates many children / and that women will give birth easily / and if it is from its fourth / it indicates much secretive unchastity and courting amongst men and women / and if it is from its tenth / it means that the women will be covered in unchastity / and much suffering of kings / and if it is that the application is from the opposition / it means that the unchaste will be harmed.

Mercury conjunct Mars indicates that people will produce fake coins / and the wise ones will be taunted / and there will be much betrayal and many deceitful people / and if it is that the application is from the third or sixth / [it] indicates that people will take it upon themselves to study alchemy / and do all things to do with fire / and if it is that the application is from the iiii. and from its iiii. [house it] indicates alchemy and secret weapons / and if it is from its x. the kings love precious stones / and become masters / and if it is that the application is from the opposition / [it] indicates that there will be deceit and falsehood amongst the people / and much theft and stabbings / and such like.

The Moon conjunct Mars / indicates false tales and bloodshed / and many lies / and people will go grey / like the wolves / and if the application is from the iii. or the vi. [it] indicates a diminishing of the laws / and it indicates that there is much meat in the taverns / and such like / and if the application is from the iiii. and from its iiii. [house it] indicates that the king oppresses his people / and if it is from the x. it indicates falsehood / and many stabbings.

Venus conjunct Sun / indicates much damage and work for pregnant women / and if it is that Mercury is conjunct Sun / it means that people are hiding wisdom and art / it also indicates many farm hands and prisoners / and that there will be much damage in alchemy as well / and if the application is from its iii. or vi. [it] indicates that the noble will be valued / and if it is from its iiii. [it] indicates work in many things / and damage as well / and if it is from its x. [it] means that the secret ones will be covered / and the laws of the kings / and if it is that it is from the opposition / it shows unanimity / and much dissension.

Mercury conjunct Venus / then secret things will be hidden / and particularly letters about goods / and the people will do common things / and have much pleasure with women / and if it is that it is from its vi. [it] indicates love and courting of women and people / in the way that they send each other letters of courtship / and such things.

The Moon conjunct Venus indicates / that people will take it upon themselves to succumb to song and debauchery / and they love good tasting things / like spices / and if it is that it is from the third or sixth / people will take it upon them to practice trickery / and like to ramble / and if it is from the fourth / and from its fourth [house] / it indicates conjugal duty[284] / and the women demand it in secrecy / and if it is from its tenth /

---

[284] *ehelich gemech*, Pfälzisches Wörterbuch defines *gemach*, *gemäch* or *gemech* as the "sexual organ (male or female)".

[it] indicates common deeds / and if it is from the opposition / women will be content with their husbands.

All these conjunctions and applications of the Planets we have spoken of / if they are seen at the beginning of the year / they will be relevant and of increased influence / and if they appear at another time / they do not possess as much force and power / than [they have] in the revolution[285] [of the year] / but if they are seen at other times / [and] neither in the revolution / nor in the revolution of the year / in its sign / then it will have little effect / Understand the root / and judge accordingly.

Of the Strength of the Planets

In the same way as you are looking before the entrance of the Sun in Aries / in the conjunction or the opposition / which Planet has greater strength in the ascendant / you shall look as well at the conjunction or opposition / before the ingress of the Sun in Cancer and in Libra and in Capricorn / and the one most equal to the first one in Aries / will increase the importance / but if it is different / it diminishes the importance[286] at the quarters / You may as well look at the conjunction or opposition / before the Sun's ingress into each sign / and combine one strength with the other / then you will find what you are looking for / but in the first place if a Planet is in the ascendant / then do not take another one / this Planet you will find to be the indicator / observe if it is good or bad / Saturn and Mars are bad / the others are good / Mercury is good with the good ones / and bad with the bad ones / Observe as well / if the indicator is rising or setting / in its epicycle / because if it is rising / and is bad / it indicates / that the things that are the basic necessities[287] / like corn and wine / and similar things / they will become expensive and valuable / but if it is setting / it is not so

---

[285] *revolutio*

[286] *bezeichenung*

[287] *notturft*, from Middle High German *nôt-durft*, one's basic needs like food, drink and basic income.

valuable / observe as well / if the Moon is increasing or decreasing in light / if he is increasing / and is carrying the bad Planet's force / then things are of high value / if he is waning / they are not as valuable / Note as well / if Saturn and Jupiter are conjunct and in a fiery sign at the beginning of the year / then things will be expensive and valuable / but if they are conjunct in an airy sign / like Libra / Aquarius and Gemini / then things are not as expensive and valuable / and if one is in a fiery sign / and the other one in an airy sign / then things are mixed up / the one that has the most dignities in the sign it is in / its strength will overtake / One should look as well / at which of the signs Saturn is in at the beginning of the year / which town or country is attributed to the sign / in this country or town / the events will manifest / Note as well / if the lowest Planets in the autumn / are under the Sun's beams / they will cause mist / and cold and moisture / but wind and clouds in winter and spring / and heat and heavy weather in the summer / lightning and thunder / if Saturn and Jupiter / and the Sun and Venus and the Dragon's Tail are together in the winter / they cause much water / causing damage / if Mars is aspecting the Sun in spring or summer / and is retrograde / it causes thunder and lightning / and heavy weather / and if it happens that Venus is forming an applying aspect with Mars / or the Moon moves from a [separating] aspect with Venus to an applying aspect with Mars / if Mercury is included / it brings wind and rain with large drops / If the Sun moves into the xvii. degree of Scorpio / and Venus is in a moist sign as well / it rains [so] that the waters will rise / if the Sun is in a moist watery sign / and Venus and the Moon are conjunct the Sun / it is raining / As well if Venus is oriental[288] in the winter / and is forwards moving / there is not much rain in the beginning of winter / and much rain at the end of winter / except / if Jupiter and Mars are close to the Sun / also if the Sun is under the rulership or dignity of Mars in the summer / this increases the heat / and reduces the cold in winter / [and] it causes dryness in autumn and spring / Saturn and Mars are dry / if they are getting together in Cancer / and the Sun or the Moon is aspecting them / or conjunct them / it indicates a dry and barren time all over the world.

---

[288] *uffgänglich*

Part Three

MUNDANE ASTROLOGY

Of Eclipses.

Rules and Indications to Judge Eclipses

Ptolemy was the nimblest[289] / [of those] whose [books] I have read / who has told about the stars / and holds in high esteem the transformation called eclipsis / darkness of Sun and Moon / and has explained it clearly in a book Quadripartito / therein is written / what each eclipse or darkness means / be it the Sun's or Moon's / and when its influence[290] is beginning / and when it is strongest / or when it ends / and it is as well written there / if the influence is good or bad / and at which country it will point or not / And if it is bad / or is indicating a destruction with death or with other things / who will be affected by it / because the destruction will either affect humans or animals / birds or fishes / or other creatures / and what humans should be watching out for / that the destruction should not affect them / and of this the other masters have written / and explained[291] it / so it may be better understood. Who wants to understand their opinion and judge on the basis of it / should memorize the rules following here.

At first one has to observe / if it is an eclipse of the Sun or of the Moon.

---

[289] *behend*

[290] *bezeichenung*

[291] Reading *erläutert* ("explained") for *geleutert*

Secondly[292] / if it is towards the east[293] or the west[294] / or the south[295] / and in which of the angles amongst the three / to which the eclipse is closest positioned.

Thirdly one should note / if the eclipse is large or small / and how long it will last / that is / how many hours it will be from the day until the end.

Fourth / One should observe / if the eclipse be of northern[296] / or if it be of southern ascent[297] / or descent[298] / because this lets one know in which region the darkness of the Sun / or the Moon will show.

Fifth / One should observe in which sign the eclipse will manifest / and in which degree / and how the Planet is positioned against the other Planet / which belongs to the sign / and how it is aspecting the sign wherein the eclipse will manifest / and how it is aspecting the ascendant and the other angles / and the twelve houses / and their Planets.

Sixth / One should note / what the sign of the ascendant is / at the time / when the eclipse is at its most advanced state / and if a good or bad Planet is therein / and how the ruler of the ascendant[299] is standing compared to the eclipse / and one shall take the sign of the ascendant[300] in its centre /

---

[292] *Zum andern*

[293] *Orient*

[294] *Occident*

[295] *Mittag*

[296] *Septentrionalis*

[297] *Meridionalis ascendens*

[298] *descendens*

[299] dominus ascendens

[300] signum ascendens

when the eclipse is fullest / that is / the time of true conjunction[301] / or true opposition.[302]

Seventh one should look for the twelve houses / which is one should divide the heaven from the rising sign / unto the north[303] / and give it three houses / and from the north unto the west[304] / which has three houses too / and from the west unto the south[305] / that has three houses too / and from the south unto the ascendant / that has three houses too / and then you have twelve houses / and one shall observe which Planets are in each house / and how dominus ascendentis and dominus loci / that is the Planet which is lord of the house / when the eclipse is forming / how it is aspected / and if it is a good Planet or a bad one / and if it is a good aspect or a bad one.

Ptolemy says as well / that the twelve signs / and the figures of the little stars next to the eclipse / should be observed as well / into which shapes they are painted or written / if it is after humans or birds / or after fishes / or after wild animals / or after domesticated animals it is shaped. Once you have observed all these things / note their meaning / which the masters have written about.

The Meaning of Eclipses

If you want to know what the meaning of each eclipse is / so observe the centre of the eclipse / this is / the time / when true conjunction or opposition[306] occurs / and which Planets are looking at it / and how they

---

[301] *vera conjunctio*

[302] *vera oppositio*

[303] *Midnight*

[304] *Occident*

[305] *Mittag*

[306] *Vera Conjiunctio odder oppositio*

are aspected / because if the Planets are bad / like Saturn and Mars / and if there are the aspects of square or opposition too / that means many evils / but if they are in a trine or sextile aspect / then the influence of the evil is not as strong / If the Planets are good / like Jupiter and Venus / it indicates good in all aspects / as long as no bad [Planet] has joined them. But when in trine or sextile aspects / they indicate more good / than in square or opposition. Now one should note / that the evil Planets are causing destruction or pollution of the air / which makes things ill / belonging to this sign. If it is Saturn / then the destruction comes from cold and wasteful mists / But if it is Mars / then the destruction comes from heat / and from bile / and from inflammation of the blood / But if it is Jupiter or Venus / they do not bring evil. If you want to know / over which things the destruction will come / so observe how the sign is built / wherein the eclipse forms / and in what formation the fixed stars are as well / which are close to the eclipse / because if they are depicting humans / like Gemini or Virgo / it will affect people / if it is formed after birds / it will affect birds / if it is formed after fishes / it will affect fishes / and the things living in water / If it is formed after wild animals / it will affect wild animals / like wolves / bears / and such like / But if it is formed after tame animals / it will affect cows and horses / and other tame animals / And Ptolemy and all the other masters are of the opinion / if it would be / that a person would eat the thing / into which the destruction has come / be it fish / meat / or bird in this person the destruction will come too / or an infirmity of days of sickness.[307] If you want to know / how important it will be so observe / if the eclipse is large / then the impact will be great as well / but if it is small / the impact will be small too. Observe as well / the colours in the eclipses / If the colour is black / green / or pale / then it indicates Saturn / but if it is red / then it is indicating Mars. Observe as well / towards which country the darkness is turned / because this country will be most affected / and the ones who are in the country towards which the brightness is facing / they will not receive any evil from it. If you want to know now / how long the influence will last / so observe / how many hours the eclipse will last from

---

[307] ... *gebreste von den siechtagen*

the beginning to the end / and observe / If it is an eclipse of the Sun / then its influence will last as many years / as there are hours [that] the eclipse will last / from the beginning to the end / But if it is an eclipse of the Moon / then the influence will last as many months / as there are hours [that] the eclipse will last / from the beginning to the end. Note as well if the Planets are stationary / which are close to it / then the influence will last longer / but if they are fast moving / then the influence will be over faster. Observe as well / that Saturn's influence lasts longer / but Mars' influence will not last long. Note as well / that Saturn influences kings / old people / and Jews / Jupiter influences dukes / bishops / and the clergy / Mars influences younger people / and warriors / The Sun influences kings as well / and mighty people / and is a helper of other Planets / Venus influences women and young people / Mercury influences scribes and advocates / and merchants / The Moon influences children and unstable people / and is a bearer of the influences of the other Planets / down onto the earth. The Planet being badly positioned during the eclipse / or badly aspecting the eclipse or the ascendant / this Planet's influence will be noticeable during the time. If you want to know / when the influence will begin / or when it will be at its greatest / or when it will end / so observe / if the eclipse is closer to the rising sign in the east[308] / or if it is closer to the setting sign in the west[309] / or if it is closer to the middle of heaven / when it is at its greatest / is the eclipse towards the east / the influence will begin soon / and in the beginning of the time / Is it towards the middle of heaven / the influence will come in the middle of the time. One should know / that the Solar eclipse influences [for] years / and the Lunar eclipse influences [for] one month / because as many hours as the Solar eclipse lasts / from the beginning to the end / the influence will last as many years / And as many hours as the Lunar eclipse lasts / the influence will last as many months. Now you know / how the eclipse of the Sun or the Moon will affect each Planet.

---

[308] Orient

[309] Occident

Of Comets

The Interpretation of Comets in Every Sign / and Angle of Heaven

When a comet is seen in the fiery triplicity / which is in Aries / Leo / Sagittarius / it means the death of great masters / lords and noblemen / and it kindles evil in evil disdainful people / and there is coming great shame and fear into the realm of Christendom / and there will be a great drought in Turkey / and there will be a lot of pain in their eyes / and there will be a great heat in summer / and there will be a great redness / which will be seen in the sky. Butzahan the wise from India said / If a comet is spotted in this triplicity / he indicates that there will be a great drought and dry time on the earth / and great damage / because / there will be a lack of the water / and great arguments in the castles and palaces / and they will be safeguarded badly / and [it] might also happen / that the king may lose them.

And if a comet is seen in the earth signs / Taurus / Virgo / and Capricorn / it means / there will be a great shortage of bread / and the earth will be dry / and the people will become very ill / because of dry illnesses / like scurf and scabies etc / and death will come amongst the cows and oxen / and other animals / and human order and laws of the people will be disturbed / and common decency / and there will be a lack of the usage of ore / like iron and copper etc / and there will be a lack in care for the earth / like tilling or planting of trees. Butzahan said / if a comet would appear in this triplicity / it creates shame / and times of drought / and this mostly when it is seen in the west.[310]

And if a comet may be seen in the signs of air / which are Gemini / Libra / Aquarius / it indicates that the air will be very dry and wispy / and burns the trees / because / it is a time of great dryness and drought / and birds will die / and people will suffer a destruction of the air / and children will die / there will be many wandering stars / and a lot of thunder will be in

---

[310] *Occident*

the sky[311] / and houses will fall / and people will die underneath them / because the houses will kill the people / and there will be strong winds / and some kings will die in the west / and there will be a lack of honey and silk / and of wool and all moist things / there will be a drought and a dryness of the soil / as well as the herbs and roots. Butzahan said / If a comet is seen in this triplicity / it means that the castles and the strongholds / and the shelters will see arguments / and blood will be shed / and damage / and cold / and hail / and some things that will come unto us.[312]

And if a comet appears in the watery signs / which are Cancer / Scorpio and Pisces / it indicates / that there will be a lot of rain / destroying houses / there will be deaths / and it will be an unfortunate year / and many losses / and much blood will be spilt on the ground / and there will be many disputes at sea / and on the shores / and there will be doubt in beliefs / and people will be murmuring between them / and between the genders / and there will be unpleasantness amongst the people / who keep up the laws of the righteous / and amongst the wise / and there will also be a war amongst them / and much poverty and much fear / and many people will die. Butzahan the wise from India said / if a comet is seen in this triplicity / it indicates / that many ships will be enemies / and they will lose people / because / many evil things will happen / and if it rises against the east / it indicates the death of members of the aristocracy / and if it is seen in the angles / the events will grow stronger and more harmful / and if it is in the west[313] / it will be weaker and smaller.

Master Albumasar says / in the book of the conjunction / If a comet is seen in the sign of Aries / it creates mental illnesses / afflicting the king of the same climate / like discord of the heart / and mistakes and quarrels /

---

[311] *lufft*

[312] ... *mancherlei zukünfftig ding*

[313] *Descendente*

which will [happen] amongst the kings of the mentioned territory[314] / and this will be seen in the Christian part of the world / and will suffer great fear / and much blood will be spilt in the places / which are ruled by Aries / like Persia / and similar places / and the king of Christendom will suffer much harm / and there will be much shame in his country / and the Turks will have many things and inconveniences[315] / and will have a time of great drought and barrenness / and they will suffer from illnesses of the eyes / and the sheep will die / and other little animals / and there will be death and discord[316] amongst the mighty rulers / and amongst the nobles / and many despicable people will rise / and evil [ones] / much gold and silver and iron ore will be discovered / and the summer will be very hot / And if it is [seen] by the oriental part / it indicates / discord between the kings of that part of the world / which is Persia / and that most of the villages of that part of the world will fall under the rule of the king of Babylonia / And if it is so that it is seen by the occidental part / it shows / that the powerful people / and the mighty / will suffer sadness / and annoyance / from the kings / and there will be a dispute amongst some from the occident / and it will rain much and the waters will overflow.

If a comet is seen in Taurus / it indicates quarrels and falls / which will occur / in the Christian part of the world / and there will be many diseases and illnesses / in the towns and villages / which are under the rulership of Taurus / and there will be a lack of bread / and the other countries will have plenty / and there will be discord in the villages / which are under the rulership of this sign / and it will come to harm through its enemies / who will point out each other's injustices / and there will be days of dry sickness in people / like scurf and scabies / and death will come amongst the cows / and there will be a lack of ore / and buildings / and in gleaning the

---

[314] *erdtrich,* from Middle High German *erderîche,* "soil", "territory" or "ground" which was seen as the opposite of heaven or of the sea.

[315] *unmuß*

[316] *misshellung*

ground[317] / and trees / and the corn will be destroyed / and will be spoilt in the climate or in the town / And if it is / that the comet appears towards the east[318] / it indicates / that the king of the climate will be frightened by his enemies / and the air will be destroyed and broken / and it will last a long time / and in the summertime illnesses and diseases will grow / and a mighty death will come amongst the cattle / and if it is towards the west[319] / there will be a lot of rain.

If a comet is seen in Gemini / it shows that the king of Christendom shall suffer from sadness / and a mighty discord will arise with the king of Egypt / and it will come to his death / and in Egypt will reign / the one who has the right / and death will come over the country / ruled by Gemini / there will be many illnesses / and the air will be destroyed / and children will hunger and die and pregnant women will die / and women whose womb is heavy / and the birds too / and it will be very hot / and hot winds will blow / they will burn trees and grass / thunder and much lightning. And if the comet is seen in the east / it means that the kings will stab / important people / and will drive them out of their places / and there will be much pestilence / like the boil[320] / and the air will be broken in the eastern country.[321] And if it is seen in the west / it shows a transformation[322] of the ways / and a robbing of the places which are under the rulership of Gemini / and there will be much rain / and much flowing of water.

---

[317] ... *zu eheren das ertrich*; *eheren* is an old expression for *Ährenlesen*, "to glean".

[318] *Orient*

[319] *Occident*

[320] Probably bubonic plague.

[321] ... *land Orient*

[322] *wandelung*

If a comet is seen in Cancer / it indicates quarrelling / death and war / and the death of many good people / and blood will be spilt / and fields will be damaged and destroyed / where people live / and there will be much rain / and a shortage of fish / and there will be war in the parts ruled by the sign of Cancer / and there will be resistance in some kingdoms / and [they] will have a new king / and he will die / and if it is towards the east / it indicates that people will commemorate in the time to come / and they will be obedient towards their King / and there will be an increase in the cost of living at the beginning of the year / more so than at the end / and if it is seen towards the west / it indicates war amongst the kings / and peace afterwards.

If a comet is seen in Leo / it shows quarrels / war and errors / which are happening amongst the kings / and that one will overcome the other at the end of the year / and much blood will be spilt in this time / in this part of the orient / and a mighty powerful person will there be / and people will get ill / of convulsive illnesses / and such diseases and pains of the belly / and many dogs will go mad / and wolves / and will die as well / and if it is seen towards the east / and the Sun is in Leo too / it will create great damage and great pain / of the water on the earth towards the west / and if it is seen towards the west / it creates great illness and many diseases / in the parts of the earth towards the north[323] / and there will be much damage amongst the biting wolves / and mad dogs.

If a comet is seen in Virgo / it shows good news for kings / who are under the rulership of Virgo / and his people / and the kings will do their people much injustice / and they will be very ill with [ritten][324] and fever[325] / and the women who are in labour / and who are pregnant will die / And will it

---

[323] *Mitnacht*

[324] *ritten* or *rit*, according to *Elsässisches Wörterbuch*: a fever of the nature of the plague, sometimes connected with the coughing up of blood.

[325] *frörer*, an old word for fever.

[be seen] towards the east / it indicates many deaths / amongst the people of this continent / whose Lord is Virgo / and one will hate the other / and if it is seen towards the west / it indicates death / coming over people / who are ruled by this sign / and lots of fruit will be growing. Butzahan said / if a comet is seen in the sign of Virgo / it means that / the enemies will rule over and dominate the kings / and the people will have illnesses in their lowest limbs / and the pregnant ones will die.

If a comet is seen in Libra / it shows the mighty power of the king's heart / in the climate which is under the lord of this sign / and that he will do many things wrong and [be] angry / and some of the occidental kings will die / and many rulers of the land / as well as mighty lords / and nobility / and much blood will be spilt / and many people will die / and it will rain only a little / and there will be strong winds / and the flowing rivers will be barren and dry / and fruit will be destroyed on the trees / and the merchants will be powerful.[326] And if it appears towards the east / it indicates that a lot of damage will be done to the king of Babylon / and the air will be destroyed / and the horses and camels will flee / and there will be an argument amongst the Christians / and they will be fighting each other / and they will receive damage from the country of Syria / And if it is [seen] towards the west / it means that the kings of this place will quarrel and fight with each other / and they will die / and kill their nearest friends / relatives[327] / and cousins / and the servants will be disobedient towards their masters / and much fruit will grow.

If a comet will be in Scorpio / it indicates much pain / that will manifest in people's kidneys / and bladders / and in secret places / and their private parts / and kings will hate each other / and women's birth rate will be poorly / and it indicates much rain / which is harmful / and the sky[328] will

---

[326] *kaufmannschatze* has a double meaning, a) "collective of merchants" or b) "merchant's goods" (literally "merchant's treasures")

[327] *moge*, from Old High German *mâg*, "relative".

[328] *lufft*

be thick and dark / and there will be much ice and frost / and hailstones / and [there will be] damage to the trees / and fish will be expensive / and there will be a lack of water / and running water / and if it is seen towards the east / it indicates / that the [people] of Babylonia will have peace / and little illness / and few people will die / and this will last 100 years / and much damage will be done by wolves / and mad dogs.

If a comet will be seen in the sign of Sagittarius / it shows that / the king wants to keep the peace / and collect many treasures / of gold and silver / and will then cast out the people / and will tell them / that they would be arrogant[329] / and will do them great injustice / and there will be much dryness / onto the part of the earth ruled by Sagittarius / and there will be destruction of the sky / and sons of some kings will die / as well as some of his noble dynasty / and horses will become malnourished in many towns and countries / and it will be very hot in summer / and there will be a lack of dates / And if it will be seen towards the east / it indicates strong and great illnesses / that will afflict or happen to the kings / and one of them will die / and the illness will last for three months / and there will be much death in the country / and there will be much killing / and fear / and there will be much bread / and much fruit on the trees / and if it is that it will be seen towards the west / it creates many memories / and useless foolish memories / and much voluptuousness caused by dreams / and women will die.

If a comet is seen in Capricorn / it shows arguments and errors / coming amongst kings / and there will be much damage for the ones in the west under their king / and war and fear / and many storms / will be seen in this climate / and towards the south / and [people] will have doubts and [there will be] madness and melancholy / mainly amongst those / who live in palaces / there will be much murder / and the paths and the streets will be destroyed / and the people who keep order will be cast out / and the people of the law / and many of the good and honest people will die / and

---

[329] Reading *hoffärtig* ("arrogant", "pretentious") for *hochfertig*

there will be much snow and hailstones / and ice on the ground / and the fruit of the trees will be destroyed / most of all saffron / And if the comet is seen towards the east / it shows that the enemies will rise against some kings / and that he will suffer and die / and the same will elevate one to be king / who will be a great master / and there will be much snow and rain / and the vines will not be harmed / And if it is seen towards the west there will be much rain / and it will be a good fruitful year.

If a comet is seen in Aquarius / it shows that some kings will die / in the east / and one will rise up / and will desire the empire / and there will be war amongst the nobles / for said reason / and many people will die / and there will be arguments in the west as well / which will last a long time / and the sky will be thick and dark with streaks and lightning / and because of the destruction of the air / many people will die / and there will be a lack of birds and fishes / and of most of the bread / And if it is appearing towards the east / it shows many thunderstorms / will come onto the world / and that the weapons of the king are kept safe / and many will be frightened many times.

If a comet is seen in the sign of Pisces / it indicates the death of important people / and mighty ones in the land of Ethiopia / which is the land of the Moors[330] / and in the land of Egypt / and many valuable people will die / and many of the mighty and the great people will die / and it will radiate throughout the world / and the kings will leave the towns because of sheer wantonness / and will burn them / and will rob and kill the people / and the clerics will fight amongst themselves / and the people will be very poor and unfortunate and [there will be] many obstacles / and sadness / and the fish will die and there will be a lack of water / and if it is that it is seen towards the east / it shows great problems amongst the judges and amongst the mighty lords / and amongst the king's servants / and they will not be subservient / and will take part of their earnings by force / and arguments

---

[330] ...*der Moren land.* From the Old High German *môr,* originally used for the people of Mauritania and later Africa.

and wrongdoings will rise up towards the east in different parts of the climates / and the people will be very afraid / and there will be much rain / and if it is seen towards the west / it indicates many memories / coming to people / and the air will be destroyed / and many people will die / mostly in the east / there will be great poverty and sadness / and this will last for three years / and the people will suffer much pain and damage / and there will be much fish / water / and birds / and that most of the explanations can be found in the chapters of the part [of the book] of the signs / wherein the comet is seen.

Rules and Instructions / to Judge Comets and their Effects

The master called Hali Abenragel says as follows / The rules that have to be known in these matters / [of] the comets / are five / The first one is / to know / why things are happening / the incident causing[331] [the] effect / The other one is / to know / in which country / or in which places / the incidents will be happening / The third is / to know / at what time the effect or incident shall be / The fourth is / to know / in which form[332] it comes / The fifth is / to know / the shape[333] it takes on / if it is good or bad.

Ptolemy the master / shows us / four shapes and movements[334] / first he shows the place / where the incident shall occur / and we shall know as well / [that] we have to turn towards the comets and signs above us / in which place they are in the zodiac / and shall look for the provinces and

---

[331] *geschicht* from *Geschehnis*, "incident".

[332] Reading *form* ("appearance") for *geschlecht* ("gender").

[333] *matteri*

[334] *moniere*, Middle High German for *rüsten*, "to mount" or "to arm", but as well related to the Middle High German word *môvieren*, "to move", (from the Latin *movere*).

countries / belonging to the comets and signs / including the triplicity / the comet is in /

And we say / that it will happen in the provinces and the same countries / we observe in the place / belonging to the sign / wherein the comet will be seen / and that we observe / the place it will have in the ascending hour / when it came into existence / or [moved] through the place of illumination / and if we find more places / in which the sign rules or judges / wherein it will be seen then / and if it is in agreement with the two aforementioned parts / then we say / that the incident will happen in the same place / you will find / to be in agreement with the sign of the comet / and if we know this / we shall look to the place / where the comet is seen on earth / and we say / that its effect will be much greater and stronger / if it is above a number of provinces or places / together with a great conjunction within the sign / and therefore it will be increased / [and] it will increase the effect of the comet / then [being in] the signs of the other provinces and places / wherein the comet may be seen /

And if it will be seen in the east / it will occur in the east / is it in the west / it will occur in the west / is it towards the south / it will be seen towards the south / and if it will be in the centre of the place / it will be large and common[335] / and it will move around a lot[336] and it will increase in half of the climates / and it will [be seen to] have the strongest incidents in places / which are towards[337] the path[338] of the comet / and in the part where it will have turned towards / that has to be understood / where the tail of the comet has turned to / there will be more damage than anywhere else.

---

[335] *gemein*

[336] *umbgehen*, "to move around", but sometimes also in the sense of a haunting.

[337] Reading *gegen* as "towards", not "against".

[338] *circle*

The third rule to give judgement from a comet is / that we know the time of the significance[339] / and how long it is going to last / that is what we may know through the following things / We have to know the hour when the comet appears / and also we want to have a look at the rising[340] of the hour / when the comet appears / in each place / and we want to set the angles / according to the height of heaven or poles[341] / like we do in the nativity / and it is clear / that the approach[342] of the comet's appearance can be manifold on earth / some are long / some wide / and according to the will [of God] they appear at the time of day or night / We shall as well know the place / where the comet will have its effect / we have to know the rising / of the hour / in which the comet began to appear / in every place / And as well how many hours the comet shines / because from the hours we will know / when the effect of the comet will set in / and from the same hours we will know / how many hours the effect will last / and from the effect at the beginning of the appearance of the comet / we know / when the effect will come or begin / and from the influence in the middle of the appearance there will be an increased effect / and from the rising at the end of the comet's appearance / we know when the effect will cease / As well we shall know which Planet is ruling during the appearance / Observe / if during its influence in the beginning various shapes and forms are ruling / we say / that at the beginning of the incident good and bad will be mixed together / and if it is / that bad luck reigns in the beginning / then the damage will be increased / and we say the same about the other incidents of the rising of the comets / and thereafter we are looking / through which hour the effect of the comet lasts in every house / and then we will know that / during such years and days / or months the influence of the comet will last / and how long it will last / and when it will be strongest / and [we will] as well

---

[339] *bedeutung*

[340] *Ascendens*

[341] *poli*

[342] *accessus*

know the location of the comet / through appearance of the angles / because the influence of the comet will be extended as much / as is the number of hours / of its extended rise.

Ptolemy / and you shall know the hours of the extension of the comet's ascension / through the rule Ptolemy has shown us in the fourth chapter of the third part of Quadripartite / wherein he says: The hours of the extension of the influence will be found / if you know / how many hours there are between the comet / and the tenth house / and the ascendant / they are six hours in time / and if you look at the hours / which are prolonged[343] from the ten hours / and after it has moved over the sixth hour / which is between the tenth hour and the influence / that makes the sum of the hours / in which the comet's rise will be prolonged / and if it has not reached the tenth / so subtract them from the six / and the prolonging of the comet remains / the beginning of the rise of the comet's appearance /

and you shall know as well / when the rise of the comet begins / as we have shown / before and after / equally / if you take the hours of the prolonging of the comet's rise / through its appearance[344] / you will know / when the centre point of the appearance will be / and if you know the hours of the prolonging of the comet's rise and its appearance / you will know / when the comet's rise comes to an end /

and if the comet will [be seen] against the eastern part of the horizon / it shows that there will be an increase in the rise in the first third / all the time [for the duration] / of the sighting of the comet / and if it is [seen] against the middle part of the heaven / it will show stronger force of the ascending in the second third / during its rise / and if it is against the west / it shows that the rise will be of greater strength / in the last third / of the influence /

---

[343] *prolongationis*

[344] *Aperitionis*

and if we want to know more about the influence / we have to know / about the increase and decrease of the separate incidents through the conjunction / and through the opposition of the Sun and the Moon / which will occur in the same place as the sighting / or in another place / which has something in common with [the first place] / and the reason why / it is influencing the former and transforms it into good and into bad / after they are ruling over the place / which they are occupying at the given time / or are relating to / But if it is that the dominator is / inferior to the one / that was dominator at the beginning of the comet's operation / or in its middle / or at its end / know that the latter will lose the virtue of the former / But if it is that the other one is stronger than the former / and because it is that they are then in a conjunction and an opposition / it will be much stronger in their eclipse / or will be increased / then because / each of them will give birth to the virtuous spirit of a great work / and if it is that it touches the other spirit / which is in agreement with the first one / their virtue will increase / and their work will be renewed / and if it so happens / that the second is moving away from the first / the virtue will be decreased / and it will be ill work / so much / that there will be a turnaround[345] / and it will be that the other one will be repulsive to the first one / and if there is more virtue / then it will destroy all the virtue inherent in the first one / and the work will be according to this one than to the other one's spirit / and in this way there are many works against us / and you have to know / that the second spirit has the ability to increase or decrease the work of the first one / but if one works at another time than the other / then nothing will be diminished nor added / and the incident or effect / is sometimes more and sometimes less / later[346] increased or decreased / and will be more or less / according to the sighting of the Planets / which are ruling at the time / being oriental or occidental / or retrograde or [in] standstill / or are fast or

---

[345] *widerkehr*

[346] Reading *spot*, as dialect for *später*, ("later"), according to *Rheinische Wörterbuch*, instead of Middle High German *spôt* for *Spott*, "derision" or "mockery".

slowly moving / and it will be judged[347] in the figures with the signs wherein the comet will be / or wherein the comet rules / together with the sign giving judgement about the future incident / and if it is that they will be oriental and standing still / there will be an increase of the incident / and if it is that they are occidental and under the Sun's rays[348] / or seen in the first night / or are retrograde / then the incident of the effect will come through them / and it is obvious as well / when the Planets have great virtues / their effect will be increased / and if they will be afflicted / they have a lack[349] in their effects / and when they are fast moving / their influence will end soon / and if they are slow[350] or late[351] / their effect will be late and slow / and if they are in the angles / their influence will be increased / and if they are setting / their strength will be affected / and if they are in the other following angles[352] / they will have middling effects in these matters / and if the comet is to the east of the Sun / the incident will be fast[353] / which will be seen / and if it is to the west / it will be more of a hindrance / and if it is so that it is diminishing fast its importance is little / and if it is lasting long / then its operation[354] is long lasting too / and its significance / and it is obvious as well / that the time of the sighting / and how long its virtue will last / and how fast it is / and slow / and its increase or decrease / according to the conjunctions and oppositions of the

---

[347] *getheilet*

[348] *Occidentalis et subradus solaribus,*

[349] *bresten*

[350] *tardy*

[351] *spot*

[352] Succedent houses

[353] *schier*

[354] *operatio*

Sun and the Moon / which will occur after the operation of the comet / which gives significance at the time of the comet's operation / and therefore you shall calculate / when the sighting will appear / and how long it will last / and then look at the others / and add to the influence / and diminish it / according to how you observe it / and according to the time you will find out / according to that it will occur.

How One Should Recognize the Effect[s] of Comets

If you want to know what the effects will be / which will occur through those things / you shall turn to their shapes and colours / and with which Planet will be combined the natural effect / of the comet / and according to the force of the Planet / ruling at the time / such an effect will happen.

The fourth quality[355] to predict / is to know / in which form[356] the sighting will be / and it can be known through the pattern of the stars / which are in the signs / wherein the places of the comets are / and in the signs wherein there are the ones / which govern and rule the sign of the comet / and the sign of the angle / which is before the comet / and what is in between.

Master Ptolemy said also / if the comets will be in human signs / which are Gemini / Virgo / Libra and Aquarius / and half of Sagittarius as well / then the incident will manifest in the human race / and if it is that they are equal to the shapes of animals / and wild animals / or equal to the four legged animals / the impact of the incident will be amongst the animals / and amongst the beasts / which are equal to them / And if it is that they are equal to crawling animals / as is Scorpio / then the incident will happen and will happen amongst the snakes / and other creeping animals / and if it is / that they are equal to animals / which are grim / like Leo / then the incident will happen and will have an effect amongst the grim animals / and if it is that they are equal to the beasts and the tame animals / like Aries / Taurus / Capricorn / and the hindquarters of Sagittarius / the effect of

---

[355] *sinne* [?]

[356] Reading *form* ("appearance") for *geschlecht* ("gender").

the sighting will be amongst the rams / and sheep / and cows / and cattle / and goats / and kids / horses and mules / and amongst donkeys / because Aries has a similarity to sheep / and the ox amongst the bulls / and the hindquarters of Sagittarius with horses / mules / and donkeys / and Capricorn is related to she-goats and billy goats / and to the roes[357] / and if it is / that the comet will be in the signs of the wild animals / as they are part of the north[358] / then they will affect the ones equal to them / and actually in the shapes / which are part of the north / meaning earthquakes / and destruction of strongholds and castles / and towns / villages / and houses /

And if it is / that the comet appears in the shapes outside of the twelve signs of the zodiac / towards the south[359] / than there will be strong winds and much rain at the time / when the governing Planets will reign / But if it is / that they will be located with the figures of flying animals / like Virgo and other figures / the incident will be [happening] amongst the birds / mostly amongst the animals / seen by people / If it is / that the comet is amongst the swimming animals / the fishes will be affected / and the other animals who live in the water / and if it is / that it will be in the figures of animals living in the sea / like crab and dolphin[360] / it will affect the animals in the sea and in places where people embark or disembark[361] /

Ptolemy says / we should know which gender the signs of the zodiac / or the pictures which are outside of the twelve signs of the zodiac towards the north[362] and the south[363] [have] / wherein the comet will appear / and how

---

[357] *raehern*

[358] *Septentrionis*

[359] *Meridian*

[360] *Delphinus*

[361] *schiffung*

[362] *Septentrio*

the sighting of the apparition of the rising of the great empire or the little empire / and about the rise of the great conjunction and the little [one] / and of the ascendant of the revolution³⁶⁴ of the year of the world / and how it is with the angles of the rise of the conjunction or opposition / which happened / before the sighting of the comet.

And if it is that somebody wonders / about the signs above us / which are not heavenly / how they might produce such great things and incidences / why one should not wonder / about the wheel / which appears through illumination / heralding wind and future rain / after the wheel has been seen / and why one does not wonder about the coming of mists and rain / after the redness will have been seen / glowing near the horizon / where the Sun rises or sets / and why one does not wonder about all natural things / which will be done in its nature / at the time which has been given to it by its nature / And why one does not wonder / about the significance of the rainbow / and other significant occurrences / seen clearly at the time / and predicting rain / and why it signifies and indicates a pure and nice time during the rain / it is because the signs above us have a meaning / and join the work of pronouncement / and it can be said of it / that all things / which are appearing / are indicating heavenly significance / because everything that is renewed in the air / the fire / the water / and in the earth / it all happens through the significance and influence of the heavenly movement at the time / of the beginning of the great / the middle / and the small / The great [ones] are the great conjunctions / and the apparitions above us / the middle ones are the eclipses / and the revolutions of the year of the world / and the four quarters of the year / and the small ones are the conjunctions and oppositions of the month / and know as well that the things appearing in the air and the fire / are following the beginning / and the movement of the Planets / where they are then / and perhaps there will

---

³⁶³ *Meridies*

³⁶⁴ *Ascendens revolutionis*

be a hidden significance / not to be understood / and feelings[365] are influencing [the] reason[ing][366] at the time of the sighting / and its sign will be seen / at the beginning of the hour / so observe / if the heavenly sighting indicates that it will rain until the fifth day / from the day of the sighting / and if a wheel is seen next to the Sun / after three days. After that the apparition of the wheel will become clearer / and makes the human understand / that rain and wind will come in two days' time / and everything will be / as it was indicated before / and it may show / or happen / what the heavenly significance indicated / in the indication at the beginning / which has been seen differently by greater people / or greater change / which has happened in some places of the world / and then / that a human would know this or the heavenly and deep meanings / he is strengthening them with the significance of the comets / which can be seen / and we may put them at the place of the heavenly significance / which will be renewed / and they themselves [are] appearing / stars / comets / if they last / and it is easier for us to make sense through them / and [to know] what shall be / and the comets and their significance are coming through the heavenly significance / like as if there is smoke rising / it is a sign / born by the smoke / and similar / are the signs above us / which will be seen through those [signs] / which are created through the heavenly will / If something appears or will be seen / of the things / which come through things / which are above us / and that / which is indicated / it shall appear / and through its will the comets have strong and heavy meaning.

Comets are not in the Firmament

All old and wise masters are in agreement / that the stars / comets / and the wandering stars / these are the other stars / called stellae secundae[367] /

---

[365] *mût*, a combination of thoughts, feelings and will

[366] *sinne*

[367] reading *stellae secundae* for *stelle secunde*,

because they are against the first natural motion / and some say / that the fiery heaven is their element / and we can not agree / that one talks about the cause of these things / because if the comets were of the fiery heaven / as they say / none of them would move upwards[368] with the movement of the firmament from the east to the west[369] / and would not have any movement / and would it be / as they say / their movement would not be true / and of a shape / and there are such wandering stars as well / like the others and they are called Asub[370] / if we see them appear / they move through the sky / and to the left and to the right / as it happens then / and obviously we observe / that more comets will be spotted / and stay in one sign throughout many days / and once we saw / that a comet appeared in the sign of Gemini / and it lasted there for many months / and did not move from the spot where it appeared / or was observed / but perhaps[371] / it was moved from the east to the west / with the movement of the circle of the xii. signs / because if it would have been of the fiery heaven / as some are saying / they would not move in this way / nor would they appear together with one figure / all the time / nor would they belong to one particular figure / But they say that there would be nine comets / The first one is called Veru / like a spit / the other Cenaculum[372] / the third Pertica[373] / the fourth Miles[374] / the fifth Domina Ascone[375] / the sixth Matrica[376] / the

---

[368] erwegen

[369] Orient zů Occident

[370] The meaning of this term is unclear.

[371] *etwan*, according to Pfälzisches Wörterbuch "perhaps", "maybe" or "probably".

[372] From the Latin for "garret" [?]

[373] From the Latin for "a long pole or staff"

[374] From the Latin for "a soldier"

seventh Argentum[377] / the eighth Rosa[378] / the ninth Niger[379] / And write [down] their customs and their ways / and their figures / and say that it is them / which shall come / if one of them is spotted / and such things are not going to be told / for something that will be born / and that appeared at one time / and not at another / and it is mainly a thing / which has one element / and will be born from it / and mix with it / And say as well / if the comets would be from the fiery heaven / why would it be more [easily] seen than the whole fire of heaven altogether / and why is it not eternal or is always appearing next to the Sun / or next to the Dragon's Head / or the Dragon's Tail / and now the tale of the sighting and influence of comets ends.

Of Shape / Size / Complexion / Colour / Nature and Significance / of each Comet

Master Ptolemy says in the last book of one hundred sayings / that the moving stars and the comets indicate a dry time / and if they will be in one part / they indicate future winds in the same part / and if it is in all parts / it indicates a lack of water / and a cloudiness of the sky / and enemies will come into the land / in the climate / where it will be seen / who will want to demand the kingdom / and contradict the laws / The bad comets are the ones / which have the xii. signs when they appear / And if it is / that Domina Cappiloru appears / which is called Dualioma in Arabic / in the corner of some realms / the king of the same realm will die / or a great master / and if it will be seen in the other following angles / many goods

---

[375] Lady / Mistress of Ascania [?] Possibly a Phrygian city. "Ascane" genitive form. (I am indebted to Sue Ward, who pointed this out to me)

[376] From the Latin for "matrix" "mother"

[377] From the Latin for "silver"

[378] From the Latin for "rose"

[379] From the Latin for "black"

will be stolen / and judges will be replaced / and if it is that it is seen in the cadent angles / the falling angles / then the king will be in sadness and pain / and will suffer great illness / and many of his people will die / in the place / where it appears / and the people will have a lack of councils.

Alchindus said / that the comet Capillorum[380] is called Domina Capillorum in Latin / and is of the complexion of the Sun / and is of pale colour / and nice appearance / and its striae[381] are stretched out like branches on a tree / and it looks similar to the branches of a palm tree / And if it appears / it indicates the death of kings / and destruction of the strongholds and castles / and death / and destruction of great people / and others of the same climate / and there will be movement from one place to another in the world. The comet / called Crinis[382] in Latin / or Domina Crinis / Duduaheba in Arabic / when it appears / it shows that one will rise up / and will be against the king / And if it is / that the comet comes from the west / and if its process[383] and movement natural / it shows that the ones / who will rise up against him / come from another climate / and if it is that it is not moving forward[384] / it shows / that the ones who will rise up / will be from the same climate. Albumasar says as well / in the book / Revolutionum annorum mundi / See in which sign the comet Crinis will be seen / and in which place of the sign / and which aspects / good or bad / the sign of the comet has / and if it is that it will be seen in the sign of a king / and that there is an aspect from the Lord of that sign / from a strong place / it indicates / that the ones / uprising against the king / will be from the same country / and will be of the king's lineage / named and recognized / and if it is / that the sign is as we have said / and there is no aspect from its

---

[380] from the Latin for "hair".

[381] *streme*

[382] probably from the Latin for "plume".

[383] *processus*

[384] ...but is of retrograde movement instead

Lord / it indicates / that it will be a great master / but as a matter of law he shall not have the empire / And in this way tell of all the signs / And if it is / that you have not understood well / what we have said before / you shall know / that the two houses of Jupiter rule over the king's sons / and the two houses of Saturn / rule over the mighty ones / and the great masters / and the two houses of Mars / and the house of the Sun over kings / and the house of the Moon / it is lower[385] / than the house of the Sun / and the house of Mercury [is] lower than Jupiter's / and the house of Venus [is] lower than the house of Mars / And this is because / the sphere of one Planet is lower[386] than the other's sphere. Master Ptolemy said / in the last word of the book of one hundred words / that the stars called comets / that have the attention of the world / are nine / and the first four are similar in colour to the stars / and all comets indicate quarrel and confusion / and death / and many dreadful things happening in the world.

And the comet called Miles / which is also named by Ptolemy / is of the complexion of Venus / and is large / equal to the Moon / and is fast moving / and has hair / and throws striae behind him / and is moving backwards through all signs / some wise masters say that the comet is called Equus / and some call it Crines[387] / that is hair / and the Master Alchindus said / that it would be a glowing star / and many striae would come from it / which are thick / and they would be like the branches of dates / and if it is visible / it creates fear / which will come amongst the kingdom / amongst kings and mighty rulers / so that all of them will be scared / and the statutes will change / and others will come larger than these / and the end will be larger in the part / where its tail is turned towards.

---

[385] *minder* ... lower in rank

[386] *niderer* ... lower in height

[387] From the Latin "crinis" for "hair" probably "lock of hair" or "plume", as in "Decrine" plumed / hairy.

A comet called Adoma / is of the same complexion as Mercury / and is small and of yellow colour / and its tail is very long / Alchindus gave it another name / and called it Decornu[388] / and said / that the comet has a raised up part / and has a broad horn underneath / and the more it rises / the more it will look like a horn / and if it is seen in the east / just as Ptolemy and Alchindus have said / it indicates a loss amongst kings / and that there will be quarrels amongst them / And if it is seen in the west / it means the same as said about the east.

Ptolemy says about the red sky at dawn or aurora / that it is of the complexion of Mars / and is red / and has a long tail[389] / and Alchindus[390] calls it the comet with the tail / and said / it would be a red star / and has a tail behind it / and some call it Decrine / and there are many saying / when it is seen / there are two signs between the comet and the Sun / and some who have not been very wise / they say / that it would be under the beams of the Sun / and make it an equal of Planets / but it is not so / because they are not stars / but they follow the stars / If one is seen in the east / and has its head facing downwards / when rising / it indicates / after what Ptolemy has said / a dry time / and many shortages in Babylonia / and Persia / and burning with fire / and war and confusion will be in the east / and damage will be in Germany / and many houses will be burnt there / and likewise there will be many houses burnt in the west / and in Egypt and in Nubia / The people from Chaldea called the comet Mutzba and said / when it is seen / it indicates a very expensive and dry time in Persia / there will be glowing and lightning / and [there] will be much damage to trees / and the king's houses will be burnt / and if it is seen in the south / it indicates that it will be bad in Egypt / and if it is that it appears in the west / bad things will happen in the west.

---

[388] From the Latin for "horned".

[389] *waedl* or *wedl*, a "fan", "tail", "twig" or "bunch"

[390] reading "Alchindus" for *Alchinns*.

Comet Argentum is of Jupiter's complexion / and is glowing / and has pretty striae / and is a little bit white / and is like pure silver colour / and it is of great clarity / so that people do not want to look at it / and if it is seen / it indicates an abundance of all good things / and that bread will be cheap in the place where it will appear / and it will mostly appear in water signs / like Cancer / Scorpio / and Pisces.

The comet called Niger / is of Saturn's complexion / and is of yellow colour / and a little bit black / and its striae are spherical / and [it] has a face or visage / but Alchindus calls the comet Demanu[391] and [he] said / that it had a little rod / and [it] has striae at the end / and when it appears / it indicates after master Ptolemy's speech / that war and quarrel will be considered / and a huge influence in the climate / where it will be seen best / and the Chaldeans call the comet Stuccelam[392] / and say when Stucella[393] appears / it indicates quarrel and war / and great influence in each town and village / and death of the king / and restraint of great masters.

The comet called Rosa / is large and spherical / and has a human face / and looks pretty / and is a little bit yellow / and its colour is like the colour of gold and the colour of silver / mixed together / and when it is spotted / it indicates that noble people will die in the climate where it is seen / and [there] will be a transformation of things in the world / and other better ones will come / and the ones from the country of Chaldea say / when the comet appears / it indicates death of the kings and the great masters / and the prisoners will be free.

The comet called Veru / is of opulent appearance / and has the shape of a sword / and has a fan moving after him / and master Alchindus says / that the comet is of red colour / and has a twig in front of him like a skewer / long and

---

[391] from the Latin "manu", a "fist" or "hand of Soldiers"

[392] perhaps from the Latin "festuca", a "piledriver" or the Latin "fistuca", a "rammer" or "mallet".

[393] As above

pointy / and is of Cauda Draconis' complexion / and Alchindus said / that the comet has two hairs or striae following it / and they are like skewers / and are of Saturn's nature / and when it appears / it indicates many bad things / and much dissension[394] / and destruction of trees / and the death of many great masters and noblemen of the east and west / and in Ethiopia / and we have not found / that Ptolemy has said / of which shape it would be / but Alchindus said / that the comet spreads out / and is like a column / rising up towards the part of the Sun / when she sets in the west / and before she rises in the east / and [it] is a star / that has two glowing branches in two separate parts / and [it is] of the nature of the Dragon's Tail / and when it is seen in the north / it indicates [a] dry time and lack of rain / and if it meets a Planet / it is meaningful / And if it is that it meets Venus / there will be a lack of water / but if it is that he meets Mercury / wise people will die / and if meets the Moon / things will be destroyed / and [there] will be a lack of wisdom / and people will have [a] great deficiency / and much will happen / and if it is that it is with Saturn or will be with him / the air of the place will be destroyed / and [there] will be quarrels / and if it is with Jupiter / it indicates great quarrels amongst kings / and that most of them will die / and if it is with Mars / there will be much quarrel / if it is with the Dragon's Tail / the Germans and the English will be destroyed by the end of March / The ones of Chaldea say / when the comet Pertica is spotted / it indicates the death of the king in this part.

The comet called Gebia / is called Cenaculum in Latin / and is of medium size / and its upper part is pointy / and it is the least spotted comet / and is not seen / only at a great conjunction / until the next great conjunction which will be in the year 960. or 1000. / And Alchindus called it the comet with the hair or Decrine / and it is called Alanoch in Arabic and [this] is the name of a big mountain / located in Persia / and there is collection of people / and the comet is big and long / and is of the nature of the Moon / and if it is spotted / it indicates damage to the laws and kingdoms / and amongst the kings ruling these kingdoms.

---

[394] *misshellung*

Part Four

WEATHER

Of Nature / and Ways of Times / and Movement of the Sun

Aries. The Sun in the first part of Aries moves rain and wind / in the middle / moderate / at the end heat and change / The northerly part is hot and destructive / The southerly is temperate.

Taurus / in the first part of Taurus the Vergilie can be seen / [they] bring violent storms / wind and mist / the middle / moist and temperately warm. The last part / where the Sucule are / stirs up thunder and lightning / with violent storms / the northerly [part] is temperate the southerly [part] unsettled.

Gemini / The Twins are moist and harmful in the beginning / the middle is temperate / the end [is] unsettled and mixed up / the northerly [part] / windy and moves brings about earthquakes. The southerly [part] / dry and hot.

Cancer / dark in the beginning / the Little Crabs[395] / are hitting the earth / the middle / temperate / [the] end / windy / the northerly and the southerly part / harmful / fiery and hot.

Leo / the beginning of the Lion / is poisonous and suffocated[396] / or airless / the middle / temperate / the end dry and harmful / the northerly part / fiery and unsettled / the southerly [part] moist.

---

[395] *die krypff*

[396] *erstruemmet*, Pfälzisches Wörterbuch: *ver-strummen*: 'ersticken', "to suffocate".

Virgo / in the beginning of the Virgin / little warm and harmful / temperate in the middle / watery / in the end / the northerly part / windy / the southerly / temperate.

Libra / in the beginning and the middle of the Scales / temperate / watery or moist at the end / the southerly [part] windy / the northerly dry and poisonous.

Scorpio / in the beginning of the Scorpion / cold / dull / snow is falling / temperate in the middle / in the southerly part warm / in the northerly [part] moist.

Sagittarius / in the first part of the Archer / hot and harmful / temperate in the middle / the end brings rain / in the northerly and southerly part / moist and harmful.

Aquarius / in the beginning of the Water-Carrier moist / the middle temperate the end windy / in the northerly part mighty heat. In the southerly [part] cold / dull and snow.

Pisces. Temperate at the beginning of the Fishes / the middle moist / the end hot / the northerly [part] windy / the southerly [part] rainy.

The interpretation above is short and [necessary] to understanding things correctly. You have to observe the Planets / particularly / the conjunction of / Jupiter and Saturn / As well as the ingress of the Sun / in Aries / Cancer / Libra / and Capricorn. As well as the conjunction and opposition of Sun and Moon / etc. And when the Sun or Moon are rising or setting / changes will be strong / when they are in the middle of the sky / they will not change anything / or do it very vehemently.

Saturn conjunct Sun or Moon indicates great changes / In winter snow / frost / cold / dullness / In summer dry heat.

Jupiter conjunct Mercury / creates wind / and increases heat / makes the air dull / makes rain but not everywhere.

Mars conjunct Venus / creates wind / thunder and lightning / Those three conjunctions are causing great changes in the sky.

Indications mentioned above / rising and setting of the signs / pictures and Planets / are not identical / in all climates and countries / which is plainly stated in Plini. lib. xviii. cap. xxvi. xxvii. xxxii.

Of the Four Seasons of the Year

There are four notable times in one year. The first one is spring / beginning on St. Peter's day before Shrove Tuesday[397] / and lasts until St. Urbanus' day / This time is naturally warm and moist / equal to air / The blood is growing at the same time / which is warm and moist too. At this time it is good to [eat and drink] / chicken / veal / lamb and eggs / [and] good wine / which is particularly healthy. The best time of the year for medication and for blood letting / because everything will be returned by the time the year has passed.

The other time is summer / hot and dry / choler is growing / the hot burned black blood / which is similar to the fire which is hot and dry too / cholerics should avoid bathing / blood letting / and all sorts of medicines / and avoid to eat and drink what is stated above. This time lasts from St. Urbanus' day until St. Bartholomeus' day.

The third time is the autumn / cold and dry / moisture called melancholia is growing / similar to the earth. Hot food and good wine are healthy at this time / medications and blood letting are appreciated / but sour drinks should be avoided / who wants to be healthy / should eat once a day in the autumn / [it] lasts from St. Bartholomei until St. Clemes' day.

The fourth time is winter / cold and moist / moisture is growing in humans / called phlegm. At this time hot things are useful / and what is spicy / and one eats more than in summer / the stomach is hottest / digestion is at its

---

[397] *Faßnacht*

best / [eat] birds and venison too. It is good for medicating and blood letting.

A human being is made of four elements / earth / water / air and fire / which the human being has most of / he will follow its nature. From the [nature of] earth / dry and cold / melancholic / heavy and of the colour of earth / similar to autumn and the nature of earth / From the [nature of] water the person is cold and moist / of white colour / phlegmatic / similar to the winter and the nature of water. From the [nature of] air he is warm and red / sanguine / resembling the glow of the nature of the air. From the [nature of] fire he is hot and dry / and is choleric / similar to the summer / and is of the nature of fire.

Dignities of the Signs

Now I will talk about the particular dignities of the Signs and Planets / Aries is cold in the east[398] / and warm in the west[399] / Taurus is tepid[400] in the east and cold in the west / Gemini is warm and moist in the east / and cold and wet in the west / Cancer is warm and dry in the east / and cold and wet in the west / Leo is warm and dry in the east / and cold and wet in the west / Virgo is tepid in the east / and cold and wet in the west / Libra is cold in the east / and tepid and wet in the west / Scorpio is warm in the east / cold and moist in the west / Sagittarius is cold and wet in the east / and warm and dry in the west / Capricorn is cold and dry in the east / and wet in the west / Aquarius and Pisces are cold and wet in the east and in the west.[401]

---

[398] *Auffgang*

[399] *Nidergang*

[400] *lawe*

[401] *occident*

It should also be understood / that when the Sun is in one of the signs / which are warm in the east[402] and cold in the west[403] / then the descriptions of the Planets and the Moon are pointing towards heat / and during the day it is hotter in the morning than in the evening / and it is similar with the other effects / If the rising sign is cold / it describes the cold [to be] more in the evening than in the morning.

Another Useful Tractate and Chapter / of Nature / Virtue and Effect / of the Twelve Signs

Each change in the air happens because of the nature of the signs / or the nature of the stars in the signs / or because of the nature of the Planets in the signs / and their aspect with the Sun or the Moon / or the movement of the Sun or the Moon towards the Planets / therefore I have firstly described the nature of the Planets / and the little stars / as they are called after the Planets and the signs / and their connection[404] and their application[405] / of this I have written three rules / which the masters put / before a change in the weather.

Aries is a sign / that naturally likes to thunder / and brings driving rain / the first ten degrees of Aries create wind and rain / the other ten degrees are moderate / the last ten degrees are hot / and cause death and destruction / The little stars which are towards the south above the line called Equinoctialis / make it cold / and the ones standing against us / that is / towards the north / make it hot.

Taurus has both natures hot and cold / but it is more inclined towards heat than cold / and the stars at the beginning of the sign / and especially the

---

[402] *orient*

[403] *occident*

[404] *zusamenfügung*

[405] *zůgang*

seven stars called Pleiades / they cause earthquakes wind and fog / the first ten degrees do this / the other ten degrees are cold and moist / the last ten degrees / are special because of Aldebaran[406] / they are fiery / hot / and bring strong weather with thunder and lightning / the stars positioned towards the south / are causing strong movement / and are of Saturn's and Mercury's nature / but the ones positioned towards the north / are fiery and are of Mars' nature.

Gemini is an air sign / and generally causes good weather / because it is of Jupiter's nature / the first ten degrees are moist / and cause [bad] weather or hail / the other x. degrees are gentle / the last ten degrees are moderate / the ones of the south are burning / the ones of the north cause wind and earthquakes.

Cancer is generally causing good weather and heat / but in the beginning / near to the stars called the Krip[407] / it causes dry air and earthquakes and strong weather with hail[stones] / the other ten degrees are gentle and clear / and [they] are of Jupiter's nature / the third ten degrees create wind / the stars towards the south and towards the north bring great heat / and are of Mars' nature.

Leo is of hot and dry nature / and causes very dull air or fog / the first x. degrees cause death and unclean air / and are of the Sun's and Mars' nature / the other x. are quite moist and of Saturn's nature / they are destructive / the southerly stars / are of the nature / of Venus and Mercury / that is very moist / the northerly stars are hot like Mars.

Virgo is a cold and dry sign / and is of Venus' and Mercury's nature / the first x. degrees cause harmful heat / the other x. degrees are moderate / the third x. degrees are cold and moist / the southerly stars are moderate / the northerly [stars] create strong winds / and sometimes death.

---

[406] Aldebaran, the orange giant star in Taurus.

[407] From *kripfen* or *gripfen*, "to grasp fast and repeatedly".

Libra is a warm and moist sign / the first x. degrees are moderate / they have Jupiter's and Venus' nature / the other ten degrees are moist and cold / like Saturn and Venus / the third are moderate / southerly [stars] are wet and cause death / northerly [stars] create strong winds.

Scorpio is a cold and wet sign / and likes to create thunder and lightning and hail / the first x. degrees cause heat and wind / the other x. degrees are moderate / the third x. degrees cause earthquakes / the southerly stars are moist / northerly ones are hot / and are of Mars' nature.

Sagittarius is hot and dry / and is a windy sign / the first x. degrees are moist [and] of Venus' nature / the other x. are moderate / the third x. are hot like Mars / the southerly [stars] are quite moist / the northerly [stars] cause strong winds.

Capricorn is an earth sign / and likes to rain / because it is the Moon's fall / the first x. degrees are hot and harmful like Mars / the other x. are moderate / the third x. make rain / the southerly stars are quite moist in moist countries / and the northerly [stars] too.

Aquarius is warm and moist / but creates cold rain / the first x. degrees are very wet / the other x. are moderate / the third x. create wind / the southerly stars create hail / the northerly [stars] create heat.

Pisces is a cold and wet sign / and is quite windy / the first x. degrees are moderate / of Venus' nature / the other x. degrees are very moist like the Moon / the third x. degrees are hot like Mars / the southerly stars are moist / the northerly [stars] are windy like Jupiter and Mercury.

Summary

These signs are particularly moist and bring rain / Cancer / Leo / Scorpio / Aquarius / Sagittarius / Pisces / and the end of Aries and Capricorn / and the beginning of Taurus / they are moist too.

Of the Influence of Planets / another useful chapter

The masters say of the Planets / that these are the Planets bringing rain / Venus / Mercury and the Moon / and the effect has to be understood / in this way / in a year when Saturn is rising without an aspect to Mars or Jupiter / it creates great cold in northerly countries / so great / that cattle and fruit will be spoilt / and it even increases if it is rising in its epicycle[408] / and if the countries are southerly / they are not as hot / as they usually tend to be / and cattle and fruit are safe / and it brings good air / When Saturn is setting / note / that the countries called southerly[409] / where the mountains are turned towards the south[410] / these are called northerly[411] / where the mountains are turned towards the north[412] / these are called easterly[413] / where the mountains are turned towards the rising Sun / these are called westerly[414] / where the mountains are turned towards the setting Sun / and note as well / that in the northerly countries many worms will be at that time.

If Saturn is moving into a hot sign / it will create great heat / if Saturn moves under the rulership of the Sun / that is between Leo and Aquarius / it creates water and floods / but if Saturn is under the rulership of the Moon / that is between Aquarius and Leo / it is barren and dry.

If Jupiter is rising in the rising sign and in its epicycle / it makes all things grow / and if it is in a sign / that depicts humans / it indicates exaltation and worthiness of people / peace and bliss / sufficiency and increase of

---

[408] *Epiciclo*

[409] *mittäglich*

[410] *Mittag*

[411] *mitnächtlich*

[412] *Norwegen*

[413] *auffgänglich*

[414] *undergänglich*

things generally needed / as Hali says / it is fortunate / and all things will be made well[415] and strengthened under its influence.

If Mars is Lord of the year / the cold of the winter will be mitigated in the north / and therefore the animals and cattle will be strengthened / as long as there are no Saturn aspects / and in summer and in hot countries / cattle and animals will be destroyed / and it will happen most when it is rising from the middle of his epicycle / and then it usually triggers war / and quick death / and suffocation / if Mars is in a hot sign / it creates great heat / and if it is in a wet sign / it creates rain / and if it is in a cold sign / its heat will be diminished[416] / and this happens mainly / if it is in a sign of its disgrace[417] / which is Cancer.

The Sun transforms the four quarters of the year according to the conjunctions and oppositions / and according to the aspects of the Planets / warm or cold / Saturn with the Sun in winter without Mars aspects / or Jupiter / increases cold / Saturn with the Sun in summer / decreases heat / Saturn works strongly in cold signs / and in autumn or winter / and Mars in hot signs in spring or summer.

Sun in Capricorn [together] with Mars / be it with aspect or conjunction[418] / makes the air milder / and causes north winds / cattle and animals will be strengthened.

If Venus is with the Sun or Lord of the year[419] / it will increase moisture and rain in winter and spring / and mostly when it is in the lowest part of its

---

[415] *beguetet*

[416] *gekränkt*, "made ill", "mortified"

[417] Mars is in his fall in Cancer.

[418] *gegenwärtig*, "present"

[419] *Dominus anni*

epicycle / and rises / and more moderate in summer and dry in the autumn / and indicates an abundance of unchastity and exuberant lovemaking.

If Mercury is with the Sun or ruling the year / it is changing the season / and pollutes it with wind and with drought / and [it] indicates subtle[ty of the] senses / and its indications are manifold.

The Moon is warm and moist in the first quarter / warm and dry in the other / cold and dry in the third / cold and wet in the fourth / and it moves across all signs in one month / and mixes the nature of the Planets throughout time / and softens and strengthens the air / that the animals and seeds will be strengthened / and the influence of the Moon is monthly / but the influence of the Sun is annual.

Of the Darkness / Brightness / and Colour of the Planets / and their Meanings / in the Change of the Air

According to these things observe the entrance of the Sun in the iiii. signs / Aries / Taurus / Libra / Capricorn / [and] which sign is ascending at the time. Observe as well the conjunction or opposition / nearest to the time of the Sun's entrance into each of the iiii. signs / and note the rising sign / and the setting in the east and the north in each country / and the Planets / which are strongest in the degree when it will be new / and keep in mind / when the Planets are shining brighter or clearer in the morning or at night / than they generally use to shine / be it in rising or setting / then they will cause change in time according to their nature / and especially if they move into one of the iiii. angles. The Moon or the circle of the Moon / if it is black or green / or large / it indicates cold air and rain / but if the Moon and the circle are clear / and is gently dissolving / it indicates clarity of the air / and nice weather / as well if there are two circles around the Moon / and [if it] turns towards red / it indicates strong wind / as well if they [are] dull and large / they indicate cold and wind / this goes for the other Planets in the same way / and as well the vii. stars called the Galina[420] / and the other

---

[420] *Hünlin*

stars as well [if they are] clear and large / it indicates much rain / but if they are clear without twinkles / they indicate nice weather / but if they are twinkling / they indicate strong winds in the summer / and cold in the winter / Note / if fiery sparks fly up and down in the sky / as if they might be little stars / if this is seen it always indicates dryness. The same goes for shooting stars / they indicate wind and dry weather / also when the sky is red at night at clear sky / it indicates death / As well a rainbow in a nice sky indicates cold / during rain it indicates warmth and nice [weather] / note as well / that a rainbow will never be higher than xlvii. degrees / and its red colour stems from the fire / its white colour from the earth / its green colour from the air / and the blue colour from the water / when the Sun moves into Aries / and Saturn is in a cold and moist sign / it indicates much rain for the year / if he is in a warm and moist sign / it indicates cold and mist / and many clouds / and if Venus and the Moon are with him / there will be much rain / If Jupiter is in cold and wet signs / it indicates gentle rains which are not harmful / and more nice weather than rain / and indicates wind from the north / as well Mars indicates heat and wind from the south / and Venus indicates rain / and Mercury wind / and the Moon rain or nice [weather] or wind / according to the nature of the one it is with or is aspecting / also the Sun when it is at her highest / and no Planet is afflicting her / she causes nice weather / but if she is at her lowest in the winter / she causes rain or snow / At the Sun's ingress into Aries or Libra / if Mars is in his own house / it causes much rain / if he is in Saturn's house / it causes little rain / he is moderate in the other signs / As well when the Moon is new or full / or is going to be full / right before the Sun's ingress into Aries or Libra / if Mars is casting an aspect from the iiii. sign or the vii.[421] sign / it causes lightning and thunder and harmful rain / As well the conjunction or opposition before the Sun's ingress into Aries / if the Moon is first aspecting Saturn and if Saturn and the Moon are in moist signs / and if Jupiter is not with them / it causes a little rain that will last long / and black clouds / but if the lowest Planets are casting aspects too / the rain will

---

[421] The author seems to refer to square (iiii.) and opposition (vii.)

be harder / and last longer / In the revolution of the year[422] / that is / when the Sun moves into Aries or into Libra / if then the lowest iii. Planets are in moist signs / then they will cause much rain / and if Mars is in Angulo terre at that time / that is / when the Sun is in an earthly sign at midnight / and if Mercury is conjunct / or iiii. or vii. signs apart from it / then it causes earthquakes and removal[423] of the air / but if Mars is in a fiery sign and in Angulo terre with Mercury / it causes great heat / which brings harm. When Mars moves into one of the iiii. houses / Aries / Cancer / Libra and Capricorn / and Venus is aspecting the Moon / and the Moon is applying to Mars in a moist sign / this causes much rain / but if Venus and the Moon are not in moist signs / then it is moderate / If the Moon aspects Venus or Mercury at the beginning of the year / and if they are both oriental[424] / that is if they are rising before the Sun in the morning / it brings much rain / but if they are occidental[425] / that is if they are setting after the Sun at night / they bring nice weather / At the beginning of the year / if the Moon is separating from Mars / it will rain the same day / in the revolution of the year[426] / that is at the beginning of the year / and if Mars is in Scorpio / and is aspecting Venus / it causes much rain / if the Sun is in Aries or Taurus / and Venus is retrograde / then spring will be very wet with much rain / if the Moon is conjunct Venus or Mercury in a moist sign / it causes rain / if the Moon is in Scorpio and Mars in Aries / it brings rain / if the Moon and Mars are in a moist sign / and Mercury or Venus are aspecting the Sun / it causes awful clouds / lightning / thunder and hail / if the Moon moves into Aquarius or Pisces / it makes the air dull / if Mercury is under the

---

[422] *revolutione anni*

[423] *entwegung* "removal" (probably in the sense of an oppressive atmosphere).

[424] *auffgenglich*, lit. "rising" or "ascending"

[425] *nidergänglich*, lit. "setting" or "descending"

[426] *revolutione anni*

Sun's beams / that is viii. degrees before or after the Sun[427] / and the Moon is in Scorpio and is aspecting Mercury / it causes rain / if Venus is in Scorpio and applies to an aspect with Mars / it causes rain / if the Sun and Venus / Mercury and the Moon are conjunct / it causes much rain / if the Moon is in Scorpio and Mars in Taurus / and the Sun in Aquarius / it will rain on that day / if the Sun moves into Libra / and Venus is conjunct the Sun in xii. degrees before or after / it brings rain / and even more when Venus is occidental / [it] brings more rain / If Venus is conjunct or opposite one of the iiii. angles / it indicates rain / at the day and hour the Moon is in a moist sign below the earth / and applies to Venus or Mercury by aspect or house / it will rain / and the rain will continue until it is overcome[428] / if the Moon is opposite the Sun / or conjunct Venus in Pisces / Aries / Libra / or in Scorpio / it causes lightning and thunder / if Venus moves into Cancer / it causes rain / if Saturn / Jupiter and Mars are together in one sign it causes rain / if the Moon applies to the Sun / it causes clouds / if Venus is there as well / then the clouds are white / and it rains softly / and it brings gentle winds / if Mercury is there / then the clouds will be differing / now red / now black / then yellow / then pale / if Saturn is there / then the clouds are black / if Jupiter is there / then the clouds are white / if Mars is there / then they are red / if the Moon is conjunct a Planet moving backwards / and the Moon is at the bottom of its epicycle / or is waxing / it indicates rain.

The Twelve Centers of the Moon

There are twelve centers[429] of the Moon / the first one is when he is with the Sun / and becomes new / the other one is / when he has moved xii. degrees

---

[427] The correct term would be "combustion". If a Planet is within 8.5 degrees of the Sun, it is said to be combust. If a Planet is between 8.5 and 17.5 degrees from the Sun, it is said to be "under the Sun's beams" or "sub radii".

[428] ...*bis er uber kompt,* ... until the Moon separates from the other Planets.

[429] *Centra*

from the place where he was new / The third is / when he is xxx. degrees from the conjunction / the fourth is xl. degrees / the fifth is xlv. degrees / the sixth is xlviii. degrees / the seventh is the opposition / and as it has been under the conjunction / it is the same at the opposition of the places. Observe the Moon / if he is in moist or in dry signs or in moderate ones / and the Planet he is with / or aspecting / and judge the weather accordingly.

Of the Opening of the Planetary Portals

Observe at the same time / if a portal has opened / if one of the lowest Planets moves towards the uppermost / and their houses are opposing each other / like the Sun moving towards Saturn / or the Moon moving towards Saturn and Mercury / and towards Jupiter / and towards Venus / and towards Mars / and therefore if the Sun moves towards Saturn / a portal opens / if Mercury moves towards Jupiter / then a portal opens / if Venus moves towards Mars / then a portal opens / Observe as well / an opening of a portal occurs / when the Moon moves from the Sun towards Saturn / or from Mercury towards Jupiter / or from Venus towards Mars / [note] as well that no other Planet is aspecting in the meantime / or that there is no Planet in conjunction with the uppermost or lowest Planet / or in any aspect / to prevent this from happening.

The four Seasons and their Properties

Spring is warm and wet / and is of Jupiter's nature / summer is dry and hot / and is of Mars' nature / autumn is cold and dry and is of Saturn's nature / winter is cold and wet and is of Venus' nature. Note as well that the quarter of heaven which extends from the rising sign up to the north is of Jupiter's nature / and the quarter which extends from the south to the setting of the Sun / is hot and dry / and of Mars' nature / the quarter between sunset and the north / is cold and dry / and is of Saturn's nature / but the one extending from the north back to the rising sign / is cold and wet / and is of Venus' nature.

Part Five

PERPETUAL CALENDAR

Claudius Ptolemy / Of Rising and Setting / Significance and Influence / of the Changes in the Sky / Throughout the Year / Every Day / the Heavenly Pictures / and their Stars.

The Days of January / Jenner or Hartmon[430]

1. On the first day the Sun begins to rise / and the days are getting longer / Eagle[431] and Crown[432] are setting / and are bringing severe weather.

2. The Sun is rising higher / the midpoint of the Crab[433] is setting / and the winds cease.

3. The remaining part of the Crab is setting / and weather and air are mixed.

4. Midwinter / the north wind is blowing steadily / Dolphin[434] and Dog[435] are rising in the morning.

---

[430] *Hartmon* or *Hartmonat*, from Old High German hertimânôt, literally translated as "hard month", indicating the hard time of winter or the hard crust of the frozen soil on the land.

[431] Aquila

[432] Corona

[433] Cancer

5. Lyra is rising / and the Eagle is setting / the Dolphin is completely visible / the winds are blowing from different directions / Pliny calls Lyra Fidicula a fiddle / it is also called Cithara a harp.

6. The Eagle is setting in the evening / the south wind is blowing from the south.

7. The north wind is blowing from the north / and northerly and easterly [winds] are [blowing] together.

8. The house of Mars / south and west [winds] are blowing together / The Sea-Goat[436] begins to rise / rainy and dark in the evening.

9. Southerly wind and rain.

10. Vehement wind from the south with rain.

11. Northerly wind with much rain and a cold violent storm.

12. Southerly wind.

13. Dark stars / Dark stars are four stars under the Great Bear[437] / two next to the Lion[438] / and four on the head of the Little Horse[439] / the first part of the Mast (a star on the ship Argo) is setting / rain in the night.

14. Dark stars / instability and change in the north-easterly / and northerly winds / the Lion is hiding / and it is raining.

---

[434] Delphinius

[435] Canis

[436] Capricorn

[437] Ursa Major

[438] Leo

[439] Equuleus

15. Northerly and north-easterly [winds] are blowing strongly.

16. Sun in the Water-Carrier[440] / [winds from the] east [and] west with rain.

17. The Harp or Lyra is beginning to set / the winds are blowing against each other.

18. The Lion and the Dolphin are setting in the morning / north-easterly and southerly [winds] are blowing against each other / and it is raining.

19. Changeable [weather] and the middle of winter.

20. North-easterly and southerly [winds] / the centre of the Crab is setting / Water-Carrier is appearing.

21. Water-Carrier is completely visible / westerly and southerly [winds] are blowing / and it is raining.

22. The Harp[441] is setting with the Crab / and it is raining in the evening.

23. East [and] north [winds] and rain.

24. Winter's day / north-easterly and south-easterly [winds] are blowing heavily.

25. Dull unsettled weather / and the aforementioned winds will blow.

26. Winter's day / the aforementioned winds are blowing / the Harp begins to set.

27. The bright and clear star on the chest of the Lion begins to set / the Harp is setting in the evening / north-easterly [winds] are blowing / some rain.

---

[440] Aquarius

[441] Lyra

A German Stargazer's Book of Astrology

28. Disgusting wind with snow.

29. The Dolphin is beginning to set.

30. The Harp is beginning to set / north-easterly [wind] is blowing strong with driving rain.

31. A mix of snow and rain.

The Days of February / Hornung[442]

1. The Dark stars can be seen / southerly and south-easterly winds are blowing / the Harp is beginning to set.

2. Heavy air / west [wind] is blowing.

3. The centre of the Lion is setting with the Harp / northerly and north-easterly [winds] are blowing.

4. The Dolphin is setting in the evening / impetuous southerly wind and rain.

5. Orion's belt (its iii. star) becomes visible dull sky and westerly wind. Orion warrior / close to the front leg of the Bull / if these stars are shining brightly / it indicates nice weather / but bad weather [if they are] dark.

6. Lyra is setting / the wind is blowing from the west.

7. Beginning of spring / west wind.

8. Westerly and north-easterly winds / are blowing.

9. Dark stars / Water-Carrier appears.

---

[442] *Hornung*, an old name for February, from the Anglo-Saxon *Horg*, for "dung" or "dirt"

10. North and west [wind] / some rain.

11. Easterly [wind] is blowing / and the Great Bear appears / Arcturus is a large star / at the end of the tail of the Great Bear / and brings bad weather in its rising. Pliny's lib. iii. cap. xxxix.

12. Winds are blowing and arguing amongst each other.

13. The Archer[443] is setting / rough bad weather.

14. The Cup or Jug[444] / a star near the back of the Snake[445] / is rising in the evening / and causes arguments and changes of the wind / southerly wind lies on top.

15. Sun is in the Fishes[446] / winter air.

16. Northerly and southerly [winds] are blowing / new Sun.

17. The Virgin[447] is setting near the Twins[448] / southerly and westerly [winds] are blowing / and north-easterly [winds].

18. The Mast[449] is setting in the evening / [a] westerly [wind] is blowing / the Virgin begins to set.

19. Northerly and southerly winds / the Mast is hidden.

---

[443] Sagittarius

[444] Crateris

[445] Hydra

[446] Pisces

[447] Virgo

[448] Gemini

[449] Malus, the mast of the ship Argo Navis, now Pyxis Nautica.

20. North [wind] with rain / the Lion is setting / the winds [called] Chelidonii are beginning to blow from the north-east for iiii. days / the swallows appear.

21. The Great Bear is beginning to disappear at around first watch / westerly wind / the night is dark and dull.

22. The days of Halcyoni. Halcyones are birds / a little bit bigger than a sparrow / with red and white feathers / a slim and long neck / and are rarely seen / Plin. Lib. x.ca.xxxii. which are laying eggs in the sand by the sea in the hardest of winter / and give birth to their young when the sea is at its roughest / which is as soon as these eggs are laid / very calm / they are hatching them for seven days / for seven days they tend to them see S. Ambr. li. ii. Hexam. These days are called Halcyonei / then the sailors like to go out to sea / because it is very calm during these xiiii. days.

23. North-westerly and northerly winds are blowing together.

24. The Water-Carrier begins to rise / winter like in the morning.

25. The Great Bear becomes visible / and it is raining.

26. The Great Bear is rising in the morning.

27. The Mast is setting in the evening.

28. Westerly [wind] is blowing / spring day.

Martius / March

1. Southerly and westerly [winds] / together

2. Vindemitor[450] becomes visible / cold northerly [wind] / the Great Bear is setting in the morning / Vindemitor / Autumn star or Grape Harvester[451] / is rising on the ii. day of March / and xx. day of September[452] / indicating early autumn and grape harvest Plin. lib. xviii. c. xxxi. and xxvi. Is close to autumn.

3. Moist air and rain / the Great Bear is rising when the Sun is at the zenith / northerly wind.

4. The Great Bear is still rising.

5. –

6. Northerly [wind] / dull / clouds.

7. Pegasus / the winged horse / is setting in the morning / northerly [wind] / the Crown is hiding in the morning / rain and water.

8. Seabirds are appearing / north-easterly / northerly wind / beginning of spring / Sun is in the centre of the Fishes[453] / Pegasus is setting.

---

[450] Ovid, Fasti 3. 407 ff (trans.Boyle): "[The constellation] Grape-Gatherer (Vindemitor) . . . Its cause, too, takes a moment to teach. Beardless Ampelos, they say, a Nympha's and a Satyrus' son, was loved by Bacchus [Dionysos] on Ismarian hills [in Thrake]. He trusted him with a vine hanging from the leaves of an elm; it is now named for the boy. The reckless youth fell picking gaudy grapes on a branch. Liber [Dionysos] lifted the lost boy to the stars." Vindemiatrix, a bright yellow star in the right wing, or right arm, of the Virgin.

[451] *Traubenleser*

[452] *Herbstmonat*

[453] Pisces

9. Miluus[454] / the Harrier[455] / is visible / southerly wind / the back of the Fishes begins to disappear in the morning.

10. The [Winged] Horse is setting in the morning / the Harrier[456] is beginning to decline / Vindemitor is setting / the Great Bear is rising / cold northerly [wind].

11. Winter is departing / north-easterly [winds] are turning around midnight.

12. The Fishes ceases to rise any further / either northerly or southerly [wind].

13. Argo / the Ship becomes visible in the evening. Westerly and southerly winds / the day moves into the tail of the Lion.

14. North-easterly [wind] is blowing all day.

15. The Horse is setting / and a cold north-easterly [wind] is blowing all day.

16. The Sun is in the Ram[457] / a westerly [wind] is blowing everywhere / storks appear / and it is possible to cross the sea.

17. Unsteady winds / [from the] north-east.

18. West [wind] is blowing / the Scales[458] are visible in the morning.

---

[454] *Miluus,* from the Latin for a "bird of prey" or the constellation "Cygnus", the Swan.

[455] *Weihe,* a harrier (genus Circus)

[456] Cygnus

[457] Aries

[458] Libra

19. North-easterly [winds] / nice [weather].

20. The Horse is setting in the morning / either north-easterly or northerly [winds].

21. The Ram is visible at times / rain or snow.

22. The Crab is rising backwards / westerly [wind].

23. Day and night are equal / rain / some thunder.

24. Northerly and north-easterly [wind] / the Horse is setting in the morning.

25. The back of the Fishes becomes visible / snow with rain / the Ram becomes visible in the morning / by the sea / unsettled sky.

26. Rain and some thunder.

27. Spring equinox / rain and some thunder.

28. The Scorpion is setting / strong winds / rain.

29. South wind and rain.

30. Violent storm / wind and rain.

Aprilis / April

1. The Scorpion is setting / the Sun makes the day a bit longer / the air is dull / northerly wind / Vergilie are beginning to rise. These are as well called Pleiades and Institor Veris / and they are seven stars on the head of the Bull / their rising indicates summer / [their] setting winter / If their descent in December is dull and dark / it indicates a wet and moist winter / if their descent is clear and bright / it indicates a dry and cold winter.

2. Misty air everywhere.

3. Vergilie / are setting in the evening.

4. South-westerly [wind].

5. West wind is blowing in the lower parts [of the country].

6. Sucule are becoming visible / and it will rain from midday / Sucule or Hyades / are the stars of the Bull[459] / If these are rising or setting it indicates rain.

7. South wind / the rest of Vergilie is setting /

8. A westerly wind begins to blow in the morning / Vergilie / are setting.

9. Waves from the sea at noon.

10. Strong and horrible north-easterly wind / rain in the evening.

11. Cold and rainy.

12. Sucule are hiding.

13. North-easterly wind is blowing / The Little Crabs are rising. In the Crab there are little stars called Aselli (Donkeys) / between them is a little space and little clouds / this is called Little Crabs.[460] Plinius lib. xviii. cap. xxxv.

14. Black / or Dark Star / wind and rain.

15. Sucule are setting / cold winds / Perseus is rising.

16. Sucule are setting / westerly wind.

17. The Sun moves into the Crab / Sucule are hiding.

---

[459] Taurus

[460] *krypffen*

18. South-westerly [wind].

19. Sucule / are setting completely / south-westerly wind / in the evening.

20. West wind.

21. Sucule are setting and it is raining.

22. Vergilie are rising / west wind.

23. Lyra appears at the time of the first torch.

24. Lyra is visible / and it is raining.

25. Little Crabs are rising / and spring is turning.

26. The head of the Bull is setting completely / and spring is turning.

27. Southerly wind.

28. A warm day with rain.

29. Hedi[461] (the little goats) are rising / Three stars in the left hand of Erichthonii / the Charioteer.[462] Southerly winds in the morning are called Hedi they bring heavy violent storms. Plinius lib. xviii. cap. xxviii.

30. The Dog[463] is setting in the evening / dull air and southerly winds / sometimes mixed with northerly [winds].

---

[461] Two stars, depicted as kid-goats, the offspring of Capella, the goat the Charioteer is carrying on his left shoulder. They are Zeta (Hoedus 1) and Eta Auriga (Hoedus 11).

[462] Auriga

[463] Canis major

Maius / May

1. The Dog is hiding / thaw is setting in.

2. Sucule are setting at the same time as the Sun.

3. Centaurus becomes visible / westerly wind.

4. The Scorpion begins to rise / northerly wind / thaw is setting in.

5. Lyra is rising in the morning.

6. The middle of the Scorpion is setting.

7. Vergilie are rising in the morning / westerly wind.

8. Beginning of summer / westerly [wind] / looking after the fields.

9. West [wind] is blowing.

10. Lyra is rising / Sucule is setting / the head of the Bull becomes visible.

11. Vergilie appear.

12. Vergilie are rising / southerly [wind] is blowing.

13. Sucule are setting / wind at midday.

14. The Scorpion is setting / Lyra is rising in the morning.

15. The Crab is rising / southerly winds.

16. Beginning of summer.

17. Procyon / the Little Dog / is setting.

18. Sun moves into the Twins.

19. Southerly wind in the evening.

20. Sucule are rising / northerly wind.

21. The Great Bear is setting / dull air.

22. The Archer is setting / southerly wind.

23. The Twins and the Eagle are rising.

24. Sucule are beginning to rise / rain.

25. Capella / the Goat / or buck / Northerly wind in the morning / it is a star on the left shoulder of Erichthonii the Charioteer [and] brings rain. Plin. lib. xviii. cap. xxvi. and cap. xxxi.

26. The Bull is setting / South and north wind.

27. Southerly wind.

28. Lyra is rising in the morning / southerly wind.

29. Strong southerly wind.

30. Vergilie are rising / heavy downpour with thunder.

31. Violent storms / winter air / heavy thunders in the evening.

Junius / Brachmon[464]

1. Sucule become visible. Southerly wind.

2. The Eagle is rising / violent storm / westerly [wind].

3. Clouds with thunder at midday.

4. Southerly wind and rain.

5. The Eagle is rising / Southerly wind and rain.

---

[464] German name for June because in three-field (crop) rotation the uncultivated field (*Brachfeld*) was worked on in that month.

6. Northerly [wind] and rain.

7. The Great Bear is setting in the morning / westerly wind.

8. The Dolphin is beginning to appear / the Great Bear is setting.

9. Northerly wind with little rain.

10. Rain in the air with thunder. Warm [and] moist.

11. Dull air with thunder.

12. Westerly / or north-westerly wind / and thunder.

13. The Dolphin becomes visible / southerly wind.

14. Orion's Shoulder[465] is elevated / it is the beginning of summer.

15. Dark stars / westerly and southerly winds.

16. Violent storms and northerly wind.

17. Westerly and southerly [winds] are blowing / Orion's Shoulder is appearing. Orion's Shoulder is a clear star / on the right shoulder of Orion. A little red.

18. Sun in the Crab / Orion is rising in the morning.

19. Southerly and westerly winds / rain and thunder.

20. Serpentarius[466] / the Serpent Holder is rising in the morning.

21. Southerly and northerly [winds] are blowing.

22. Orion is rising.

---

[465] Betelgeuse

[466] Ophiuchus

23. Dark stars are rising / it is getting warmer.

24. South corner[467] / snail[468] / stormy air.

25. South-westerly and westerly winds.

26. The night is shortest / Orion is rising.

27. Rain in the evening / the Dog becomes visible.

28. Winds are fighting.

29. The Dog is rising in the morning / Orion's belt is appearing. Orion's belt consists of the three stars / in the centre of Orion.

30. The Great Bear is setting in the morning / violent storms.

July / Hewmon[469]

1. Dull air because of northerly wind.

2. Dark stars / southerly or westerly winds.

3. Moist dull air.

4. Orion is rising / Orion. Stork is setting / southerly wind brings many violent storms / like Arcturus[470] and Hedi. Plinius lib. xviii. xxviii.

5. The centre of the Crab is rising / southerly and north-easterly winds.

---

[467] *Mittaglicher angel* [?]

[468] *schnel*

[469] Heumonat, the month for making hay.

[470] Reading "Arcturus" for *Acturus*.

6. Estesie / Estesie are north-easterly winds / they blow for xl. days / in July[471] and the dog days[472] / Plin. lib. ii. cap. xlix. and lib. xviii. cap. xxiiii.

7. The Crown is setting in the morning / southerly wind.

8. Cepheus is rising / violent storms around midday.

9. Orion is completely visible / southerly wind.

10. Estesie Prodromi / north-easterly wind. [It] is blowing eight days before the dog days. Plinius lib. ii. cap. xlix. Forerunner of the dog days.

11. Downpours with thunder / northerly [wind].

12. Orion is rising completely in the morning / the Forerunner [Prodromus] is blowing strong from the north-east.

13. South-westerly wind / dissonance.

14. North-easterly wind.

15. Canicula / the little dog is rising / Estesie are blowing from the north-east.

16. Orion is rising / north-easterly wind / dissonance.

17. Middle of summer / cold days from north-east.

18. Westerly wind / sometimes southerly / the Dog is rising in the morning. Estesie are blowing strong from the north-east.

19. Orion is rising / south-easterly [winds] / Orion can be seen completely.

---

[471] *Hew mon*

[472] *Hundstag*

20. Sun in the Lion[473] / south-easterly wind / the Dog is rising.

21. Estesie together with other winds / are blowing for xxi. days.

22. The Forerunners are blowing everywhere.

23. The whole of the Crab is rising together with the Lion / the Eagle is setting.

24. The Lion is rising together with the Sun and with the Dog / the Crab is descending.

25. The Twins are beginning to set / the Dog becomes visible / southerly wind.

26. Sandy or dusty / dry air / the Eagle is setting / the Lion is rising / southerly wind.

27. Dog / heat.

28. Strong heat / Estesie are blowing heavily.

29. The clear star in the Lion's chest is rising / cold northerly [wind] because of the heat.

30. Autumn fruits are becoming visible / the Eagle is setting in the morning / dull air.

31. Southerly and south-westerly [winds] are blowing together.

---

[473] Leo

Augustus / August / Erndmon[474]

1. The Eagle is setting in the morning / south-westerly [wind] / dry heat.

2. The Eagle is setting / air from the south.

3. Warm / moist.

4. The centre of the Lion is appearing / The Mast is visible in the next two days / southerly [wind] / with driving rain.

5. The Crown is setting / the centre of the Lion is rising / strong southerly wind / cranes are beginning to appear.

6. Lyra is completely visible / heat at midday.

7. The centre of Orion is hiding / dull days because of southerly wind / but hot.

8. The Lion is rising / unbearable heat / dull air / the centre or girdle of Orion is rising.

9. Dark stars / northerly wind is blowing gently / medium heat.

10. A lunar eclipse is taking place around this day / southerly and northerly winds are blowing / great heat.

11. Lyra is setting in the morning / autumn begins / the winds are meeting each other.

12. The winds are quarrelling and fighting with each other.

13. The Dolphin is setting in the morning.

14. Beginning of autumn.

---

[474] *Erndmon*, the month of the harvest

15. Lyra is setting / northerly wind.

16. The Dolphin is hiding / medium heat.

17. Lyra is setting in the morning / Sun moves into the Virgin / southerly wind rain and thunder.

18. The Sun is completely in the Virgin.

19. The Virgin is rising.

20. A northerly wind is blowing gently / the Virgin is rising completely / good weather.

21. The Virgin is rising / northerly wind.

22. Estesie are calming down / a cold north wind is beginning to blow.

23. Dolphin is rising / southerly wind.

24. Vindemitor becomes visible / south and west winds are blowing together. Plinius says that Vindemitor xi. cap. September / would rise / on the xx. of the Herbstmon.

25. The Virgin is beginning to appear.

26. A westerly wind is blowing gently.

27. The Virgin is rising / a westerly wind is blowing gently.

28. Andromeda is rising.

September / Herbstmon[475]

1. The Fishes towards the south. Cetus or Motius. Is not hiding any more.

---

[475] *Herbstmon*, the month of autumn.

2. Thunder and rain.

3. The Great Bear is rising together with the Vindemitor / the Mast is hiding.

4. House of Mercury / westerly wind / unsettled winds bring rain.

5. Pegasus / the horse is rising.

6. The Goat becomes visible / south westerly [wind] is blowing / rain in the evening.

7. The Great Bear is appearing / north-easterly [wind] is blowing / some thunder.

8. The centre of the Virgin is rising / westerly and southerly winds are blowing.

9. Sky as above.

10. Sky as above.

11. The Great Bear is rising.

12. When the Great Bear is rising it rains.

13. Vergilie are rising together with Pegasus.

14. The swallows cannot be seen anymore / the Goat is rising / rain.

15. The xii. part of autumn begins.

16. A westerly [wind] is blowing everywhere with south westerly [wind].

17. The Fishes are rising / northerly [wind] is calming down.

18. Sun in the Scales. The Cup / or the Bowl is appearing / the middle or the centre of the Great Bear is visible in the morning.

19. When the Great Bear is rising it will rain abundantly.

20. Day and night are equal in autumn / The Fishes are setting.

21. Argo / the Ship / is descending / dull rainy sky.

22. The Fishes are setting / rain from the south / impetuous air and wind / violent storms at sea.

23. A lunar eclipse tends to happen around this day / Centaurus is rising.

24. Dull and impetuous air.

25. The Hedi (the little goats) are rising / strong southerly wind.

26. The Virgin is not rising any more / Vergilie are visible in the morning and evening / the Hedi are rising together with the Sun / strong winds and waves at sea.

27. Strong southerly wind / terribly violent storms.

28. Vergilie can be seen in the morning / rain and southerly wind.

29. The Little Goat is becoming visible / when the Vergilie are setting in the evening.

October / Wine Month

1. Vergilie are becoming visible as they rise / southerly [wind] is blowing in the morning.

2. Southerly wind and rising of the Vergilie.

3. Heniochus[476] / the Charioteer is setting and [it] is thundering from midnight.

---

[476] *Heniochus*, Latin transcription of the Greek title for Auriga, "Eniochos".

4. Hedi are rising / rain.

5. The Crown becomes visible.

6. The centre of the Ram is setting with the Scorpion.

7. As above.

8. The Crown is rising together with the Hedi. Dull sky.

9. The Hedi and the Vergilie are visible / south-westerly wind.

10. The Scales beginning to rise / westerly [wind].

11. The Crown is rising in the morning / the winds are turning / winter like violent storms out at sea.

12. The Vergilie are rising / southerly wind.

13. The Crown becomes visible / change in the air / violent storms.

14. A north-easterly [wind] is blowing strong.

15. The middle of autumn / southerly wind.

16. Orion is visible / dew or hoar frost.

17. Weather as stated above.

18. A sad dull day.

19. Sun is in the Scorpion / westerly wind.

20. Vergilie are setting / dull unsettled air.

21. As stated above / rain.

22. The tail of the Bull is setting / southerly wind with rain.

23. Scorpius is setting / north-easterly [wind] / and terrible violent storms out at sea.

24. Vergilie are setting.

25. Centaurus is setting in the morning.

26. Half of the tail of Scorpio is setting.

27. Sucule are setting / cold north-easterly [wind] / raw winter like air out at sea.

28. Vergilie and Orion are setting completely.

29. The Great Bear is hiding. Strong winds.

30. Cassiopeia is beginning to hide.

31. Orion and the Eagle / are setting completely in the evening / Lyra is rising.

November / Winter Month

1. Vergilie are setting / frost in the morning / the Great Bear is hiding. The air is changing towards cold.

2. Cold winds and rain.

3. Lyra is rising in the morning / north-easterly [wind].

4. South and west wind / much rain.

5. Lyra appears at the time the Sun rises / north-easterly [wind].

6. The Great Bear is setting in the morning / dull air and fog.

7. Vergilie and Orion are hiding / north-easterly [wind].

8. Dull and dismal air.

9. The clear star[477] Scorpionis[478] and winter sting.[479]

10. Beginning of winter.

11. Vergilie are hiding.

12. The central star Scorpionis is becoming visible.

13. Vergilie and Orion are setting in the morning.

14. Scorpius is setting in the morning.

15. Lyra is rising in the morning / south-easterly [wind] / south and north-easterly [winds] / are blowing together.

16. Weather as above.

17. A mixed day / southerly wind.

18. Sun is in the Archer. Orion is rising together with Lyra / violent storms.

19. The horn of the Bull is setting together with the Sun / north-easterly [wind].

20. Terrifyingly violent storms.

21. Sucule are setting together with the Hare[480] in the morning.

22. Cold rain.

---

[477] *Clar gestern* [?]

[478] Antares

[479] *angel*, (Stachel), from Old High German angul, "sting". Perhaps Lesath, or Lesuth, "the sting", although sources seem to have different opinions about its placement.

[480] Lepus

23. The horns of the Bull are setting.

24. Beginning of winter / it is beginning to get cold and cold dews are falling.

25. The Sun is in the first part of the Archer.

26. Interpretation and weather as above.

27. The Dog is setting / air from the south and rain.

28. The Dog is beginning to hide / a misty day.

29. The Dog is setting in the morning / south-westerly [wind] and rain.

30. Orion is setting / westerly / south-westerly [wind] and rain.

December / Month of Christ

1. Dull air. Northerly [wind] / the whole of Orion is setting in the morning.

2. The Dog is setting / northerly [wind] in the evening.

3. Violent storms with clouds.

4. The Archer is setting / and north-easterly [wind].

5. Rain all day long / and north-easterly [wind].

6. The centre of the Scorpion is becoming visible.

7. The Eagle is rising / south-westerly [wind].

8. The Scorpion is completely visible.

9. The Dog is rising in the morning / southerly wind.

10. Strong north-easterly [wind] / dark sky with violent storms.

11. Dark stars / north / and north-easterly [winds] / blowing.

12. First north-easterly / then south [wind] with heavy rain.

13. The whole of the Scorpion is rising / south and north-easterly [winds] are blowing and it is raining.

14. The little Goat[481] is setting.

15. South and north-easterly [winds] are blowing / dull air and mixed thunderstorms.

16. Weather as above.

17. The Sun is in the Sea-Goat.

18. Dark stars / the winds are fighting amongst each other.

19. The little Goat is rising.

20. The Eagle is rising in the evening.

21. North-easterly [wind] is beginning to blow / afterwards south wind the whole day.

22. The Eagle is rising in the evening.

23. The little Goat is visible in the morning / so far [according to] Ptolemy.

Explanation of the Things Mentioned Above. D. Hieronymi Cardani / Medici Mediolanen.[482]

Orion / Great Bear / and Crown / bring violent storms when they rise.

---

[481] Capella

[482] Gerolamo Cardano, the Milanese physician.

The Hedi / little Goats and the Goat next to the Charioteer bring wind.

The Hiades or Sucule / bring rain.

The setting of the Vergilie leaves the weather as they find it.

The first part of the Lion and the two Dogs / bring heat.

Part Six

ASTRONOMY

Explanation of the Spheres

Explanation of the Spheres and Circles of Heaven

There are ix. heavens on top of each other / which are all moveable and are rotating daily around the world / And above the ix. heaven is the x. heaven / which is quiet and motionless and is called Caelum cristallinum[483] which is the crystalline heaven / or called Caelu[m][484] empireu[m] / that is the emperor's heaven / not that it is made of crystal or of emperors / but because of the width and clarity there / it is called thus / and it is thought that God and his chosen friends are living there.

The ninth heaven is called primum mobile / that is the first mobile heaven / it is also called Mona sphera / that is the ix. sphere / or the ix. circuit / in this heaven there is no star / but therein is a wide path or a wide circle called zodiacus / and this circle is not running right or equal from dawn towards dusk / but it is obliquely[485] in the sky / and the same zodiac / half of it is towards the north[486] / and the other half is turned towards the

---

[483] Reading *Caelum* for *Celum*

[484] Ibid.

[485] *zwerchs*, according to the *Pfälzische Wörterbuch* a regional expression for *schräg*, "tilted" or *quer*, "across", "transversely".

[486] *norwegen*

south[487] / and this path is divided into xii. parts / these are the xii. signs / and as it is divided into xii. parts across the length / it is also divided into xii. parts in its breadths / and there is a circle which is running straight through the middle of the zodiac which is called via solis / this is the path of the Sun / the Sun never leaves this path neither to the right nor the left hand side / this path is also called linea ecliptica / this is the line wherein / or where eclipses of the Sun and the Moon are occurring / and nowhere else. The width of the zodiac / which is turned from the Sun towards the north[488] / has a width of vi. degrees / and imagine if there would be vi. circles moving alongside the Sun's path / around and around in the sky / these vi. circles are called paralleli / and as well the width of the zodiac which is turned from the Sun's path towards the south[489] is vi. degrees in width and has as well vi. circles alongside the Sun's path which are called paralleli / and all Planets move along these xii. circles / so they are sometimes inside the path of the Sun towards the south / and sometimes they are outside the Sun's path towards the north / but the Sun will always stay in the middle / The width which is facing away from the Sun towards north / is called northern latitude[490] / this is the width of the zodiac / facing towards the north / but the width which is inside[491] the Sun's path is called southern latitude[492] / this is the width of the zodiac / facing towards the south / There is a circle through the zodiac / and this is the path all the Planets take away from the Sun towards the north / and back again to the Sun towards the south of us / and then further inside the Sun's path / and the circumference is divided into xii. signs / there are two from the

---

[487] *mittag*

[488] *norwegen*

[489] *mittag*

[490] *latitudo septentrionalis*

[491] *hinsit*

[492] *latitudo meridionalis*

beginning of the Sun's path / up to the sixth parallel towards the north / There are iii. signs back to the Sun's path / There are ii. signs from there towards the south / up to the sixth parallel / and then three signs back to the Sun's path again / If there is a Planet in the three signs of the circle / which are facing towards the north / then the Planet is called northern ascending[493] / which means that he is turned towards the north / and is rising / but if the Planet is in the other three signs / he is called northern descending[494] / he is dropping / But if a Planet is in the three signs which are facing towards the south of the Sun / so the Planet is called southern ascending[495] / from there back into the Sun's path / the Planets are called southern descending[496] / and the xii. signs are called argument of latitude[497] / and begin in the Sun's path. If the Planet moves from south to north / if he then crosses the Sun's path / this crossing is called the Dragon's head / and if he descends again after the vi. sign towards the south / but moves against the Sun's path / this crossing is called the Dragon's tail.

Another Explanation of the Spheres and Circles of Heaven

There are nine spheres of heaven which are moveable / and the first or uppermost is called Primum Mobile / or the ninth sphere / that is the first

---

[493] *septentrionalis ascendens*

[494] *septentrionalis descendens*

[495] *meridionalis ascendens*

[496] *meridionalis descendens*

[497] *agrumentum latitudinis*, reading *argumentum latitudinis*, the argument of latitude. "If the mean motion ☊ should be added to the mean motion of Luna, the mean motion of Luna from the Node ☊ will be had, which is also called Argument of Latitude"(Gregory, David: *Astronomiae Physicae & Geometricae Elementa*, 1726, pxxi)

moveable one / therein is a circle which is oblique[498] and wide / is called zodiac / its length is divided into twelve signs / and the signs begin with Aries. The width of the circle is divided into degrees / and each sign of the length of the zodiac is divided into thirty degrees / and each degree in lx. minutes / The middle of the width of the zodiac circle is called the line of the ecliptic[499] / because eclipses of the Sun or Moon are happening therein or thereby / it is as well called via solis / that is the Sun's path / because the Sun moves on this path all the time and never gets out of it / neither to the right nor to the left side / but the other Planets are sometimes moving off the same line six degrees towards the south[500] / or six degrees towards the north[501] / some even more / some less.

All the other spheres are moving below these ix. spheres and below the zodiac / the viii. sphere with the common stars[502] / and below it moves the vii. sphere with Saturn / below it moves the vi. sphere with Jupiter / below it moves the v. sphere with Mars / below it moves the iiii. sphere with the Sun / below it moves the third sphere with Venus / below it moves the other sphere with Mercury / below it is the circle of the Moon.

It has to be noted that all Planets have epicycles / which means smaller circles. The centres are always on the Sun's path / and the movement of the centre of each Planet's epicycle / is called [the] deferent[503] of the Planet / and this movement is always steadily against the firmament through the xii.

---

[498] *zwerchs,* according to Pfälzisches Wörterbuch for *quer,* "across" or *schräg* "oblique", "askew".

[499] *linea Ecliptica*

[500] *Mittag*

[501] *Norwegen*

[502] That is the fixed stars

[503] *mittellauf*

signs / in one day as much as in any other. The Planet's movement in the epicycle / that is in the small circle is not always the same / because at one time it moves lesser / than at another time / and sometimes it rises in the epicycle / and sometimes falls / and therefore as the length of the zodiac is separated into xii. signs / each epicycle is divided into twelve signs too / and each sign into thirty degrees / and each degree into sixty minutes / and the division of the epicycle is called [the] argument[504] of the Planet's epicycle / to know in which place of the epicycle the Planet is standing / If you find in the argument[505] no sign / no degree / no minute / the Planet is in auge / that is / on the uppermost part of the epicycle / and is far away[506] from the Earth[507] / and it is called directus / which is moving forward. But if you find three signs / then the irregular movement of the Planet goes forwards / and the deferent backwards / then the Planet is called stationarius descendens / which means that the Planet is stationary and descending in the epicycle. But if you find six signs / in argument / then the Planet is at the lowest point on the epicycle / and is close to the Earth / and is retrograde / meaning / it moves backwards. But if you find nine signs in the argument / then the Planet is stationarius ascendens / that is / it is stationary and ascending / and then the deferent of the Planet is earlier than the irregular movement /

But it is different with the Moon / because the Moon / when he is in the uppermost part of his epicycle and descending / he is moving against sunset / when he is at the bottom of his epicycle and rises / he is moving against sunrise / and therefore if there is in the argument of the Moon no sign / no degree / no minute / then the Moon is on the top of his epicycle / and is moving daily. But if there are three signs in the argument / the Moon

---

[504] *argumentum*

[505] *argumento*

[506] *vert*, Middle High German for "far away"

[507] The apogee of the deferent.

is descending / and the irregular movement is later than the deferent. But if you find six signs in argument / so the Moon is low on his epicycle / and is close to the Earth / and is moving fast / and moves fourteen or fifteen degrees per day. But if there are nine signs in the argument / the Moon is rising / and faces the orient / and then the irregular movement is earlier than the deferent.

Now note / if you want to know the deferent of a Planet / so find his root first / which is made for the year of Christ / and write it down on a board / and then look for the day of the month / of which you want to know the deferent of the Planet / and what you find for sign / degree and minute / write below the root / like sign below sign / degree below degree / minute below minute / after that add it all / and begin with the minutes / and add the minutes of the day you were looking for / to the minutes of the root / and add the degrees to the degrees / and the signs to the signs / and if it is that the addition of the minutes / results in more than sixty / so add one degree for the sixty minutes to the degrees / and keep the minutes left over / After that add degrees to degrees / and if there are more than thirty degrees / make a sign out of it and add it to the first sign / and keep the degrees left over / and as often as you have twelve signs / discard them / and keep what is left over of the signs / and if nothing is left / so write the number / 0 / which indicates nothing / what is left of signs / degrees / and minutes / that is the deferent of the Planet / the deferent you have been looking for / and it is for the midday of the same day / you were looking for.

But if you want to know its deferent at another hour / so note how many hours have past since midday / and look for the hour in the tables of the hours of the Planet's deferent[508] / and what you will find / you add to the deferent / which you have found / for midday / and subtract as many degrees and minutes / as you find in the tables of the hours / this gives you the deferent for any hour you want.

---

[508] An example of such tables is given in Appendix B.

A German Stargazer's Book of Astrology

If you want to know when it will be new after the deferent / so look for the deferent application of the Moon to the Sun[509] / in the tables with the roots / and with the day of the month closest to the new / which you want to know / in the same way as it has been written about the Planets before / and what you will find / of signs / degrees / minutes and seconds / write on a board / and transform it into days / hours / minutes and seconds / and also go to the first one[510] with the signs / and mark[511] in the table of transformations of the applications of the signs[512] / and what you will find there of sign / day / hour / minute or second / that write / to the first / sign below sign / day below day / hour below hour / minute below minute / second below second / then continue[513] with the minutes / then continue with the seconds from the tables of the seconds / and then do as you have done before / that is / write day below day / second below second / then add it up / as well / write seconds to seconds / and if there are ever more than sixty / so make minute out of sixty / and keep the rest / then add minutes to minutes / and if there are more than sixty / so make an hour out of sixty / and keep the rest / and then add the hour to the hours / and if there are more than twenty four / so make one day out of the twenty four / and keep the rest / and what you will find afterwards of days / hours / and minutes / and seconds / that add to the midday / you were looking for / and you will have the time of the new deferent.

And this is done for the town of Strasbourg / but who wants to transfer it to another place / has to look at the table / country and place / and if it is /

---

[509] *Applicationis Lune ad Solen*

[510] Presumably the first table, although no tables were included in the printed text. See Appendix B for more information on these missing tables.

[511] *zeichnen*

[512] *signorum applicationis*

[513] *gang ein*

that the place or country is located more towards the east⁵¹⁴ / and has more degrees of longitude than Strasbourg / so observe how many more degrees there are / so subtract four minutes for each degree / of the roots / and for xv. degrees subtract one hour / But if the place or country is located more towards the west⁵¹⁵ / so add the same / but in the roots of the applications⁵¹⁶ / you have to add iii. minutes to the motion / and if it is towards the west / one has to subtract four minutes.

Meaning and Height of the Spheres

The aforementioned masters tell us / the idea of [the size of] heaven is 54,000 stadia / and therefore there are lxx. stadia on Earth for each degree in the heavens. Now there are 360 degrees in the whole of heaven / that makes 31500. miles towards the Sun. Note / that one stadium is one eighths of a mile / Ptolemy and Alfraganus say / that the diameter of the Earth would be 6500. miles. Imagine in your mind a round circle / it may be large or small / therein see a line from one end / to the other / which [separates] this circle into equal parts / in length and width / which is called diameter. The master teaches in the Sphere / that the Moon decreases along the same lines of each circle / the xxii. part of the whole circle / therefore the third part of it / which remains is the line / which is called diameter. Hell is in the centre of the Earth / therefore it is 3250 miles from the upper part of the Earth / because it is in the centre of the line called diameter. Note once you grasp with your intellect or mind a point in the middle of the Earth / which is equal to all parts of the Earth / in length and width / this point is called centre. Alfraganus tells us that the closest distance of the Moon from the Earth is 9137. miles / and half a mile / but the longest distance of the Moon / which is closest to Mercury / it is 8742. miles / the furthest distance of Mars / which is like the closest distance of Venus is 42350. miles away from

---

⁵¹⁴ *Orient*

⁵¹⁵ *Occident*

⁵¹⁶ *Applicationis*

the Earth / the furthest distance of Venus / which is closest to the Sun / is 3090000. miles from the Earth / the furthest distance of the Sun / which is closest to Mars / is 1465500. miles from the Earth. The furthest distance of Mars / which is closest to Jupiter / is 280447800. miles from the Earth. The furthest distance of Jupiter / which is closest to Saturn is 46816250. miles away from the Earth. The furthest distance of Saturn is equal to the distance of the immobile sphere / which is 65357500. miles. The point of heaven called axis is / 14120000. miles. The size of the heaven with stars 50189196. miles. Each degree of the circle called zodiac has 540062. miles. Note / that zodiac / is Latin for sign bearer / but in the Greek language it is called a life / because all things on Earth / through the power of the Sun / moving in a circle / have their life. Aristotle observes / that through rising and setting of this circle / things on Earth will be born and destroyed / or it is called zodiac because / there are twelve signs in the circle / which are equal to the qualities of the twelve animals / which are / Aries / Taurus / Gemini / Cancer / Leo / Virgo / Libra / Scorpio / Sagittarius / Capricorn / Aquarius / Pisces. In these signs the Sun moves through the months / in the way / that she moves into one sign in one month / and into another one in another month / and most noticeably she moves into another sign in the middle of the month. One degree is the thirtieth part of a sign / and what is called a natural day is fourteen hours long.[517]

Size of the Planets above the Earth

The measure of the body of the Sun is 166 times bigger than the whole of the Earth / the measure of the body of the Moon is xxxix. times as big / as the whole of the Earth / the body of Mercury is one 22090. part of the body of the Earth / the body of Venus is one xxxiiii. of the body of the Earth / The body of Mars is equal to the Earth one time / and half a time / and the average of the eighth part of one part / the body of Jupiter is equal to the Earth xiiii. times / Saturn's size is equal to the Earth times ten / Therefore all Planets are bigger than the Earth / as has been stated above.

---

[517] It should, of course, read "twenty four", as is rightly stated in another portion of the text.

Size of the Fixed Stars

The wise masters tried to divide into six parts the fixed stars / as much as it was possible with their instruments / in this way / In magnitudine Prima / that is in the first magnitude / there are xv. stars / and each of them is 107. times bigger than the Earth / In the other magnitude are xiv. stars / each is nine times the size of the Earth / In the third [magnitude] are 208. where each is lxxii times bigger than / the Earth / In the fourth [magnitude] 474 each is like the Earth liiii. times / In the fifth [magnitude] 217. there each is like the Earth xxxvi. times / in the sixth [magnitude] lxiii. and the smallest amongst them is twenty times bigger than the Earth. The size of the other fixed stars / which are all invisible / is xviii. times that of the Earth.

Note / Alfraganus says in the book which is called / De Spheris[518] / that the word magnitude / according to its definition is each thing / which one wants to measure in length / breadth / and width. Amongst all stars the Sun is the largest / and there are xv. stars of the first magnitude / called the Prima magnitudine / thereafter Jupiter / thereafter Saturn / thereafter all fixed stars according to their order / thereafter Mars / thereafter the Earth / thereafter Venus / thereafter the Moon / Mercury for the tenth time. The starry heaven is moved from rising to setting in each year / and to the rise again 355. times / and is in a quarter of one day / that is once in twenty four hours / which is called a natural day / and the sum[519] of all days of the year is 365. days / and one quarter of a day or six hours / if one adds these / there will be a leap year in the fourth year / And the movement of the heaven / that is starry / is called the daily movement / and the same heaven is moved in one hundred years / one degree against the movement of the lower heaven / this movement will be completed in 36000. years / and that is called the great year / as one knows who is counting according

---

[518] Alfraganus' work is called *Elementa Astronomica*, it is Sacrobosco's work which is entitled *De Spheris*.

[519] Reading *Summe* ("sum") for *Sonne* ("Sun")

to arithmetic[520] / because that many degrees are in the circle [of the] zodiac / no more and no less / this will be understandable / if one divides twelve times thirty degrees / and twelve signs are in the circle called zodiac / and each sign has thirty degrees.

The Eighth Heaven

The eighth heaven is carrying the small stars or the common stars / which are called fixed stars[521] / and this heaven with the stars circulates around the Earth together with the ninth heaven / from rising until setting / and this movement is called Motus Raptus [text on right margin: Motus Raptus / a coerced and forced move] / it is moving against the ninth heaven below the zodiac in 120 years one degree / in this heaven there are many stars whose nature is equal to the Planet's nature / and therefore when the Planets join the stars of their nature / than they have twice the strength / Ptolemy writes in *Quadripartito* / that the twelve signs have mighty powers from the common stars which are in them / and one has to realize / that the heavenly signs have a different effect in our time / than they had in Ptolemy's time compared to our time which is the year 1410 a.d. / xxv degrees and more / and therefore are now the stars in Aries / which were in Pisces at the time / and as well are now the stars in Aries / which were in Pisces at the time / and the ones that were in Aries are now in Taurus / and so forth through the twelve signs / Whoever wants to know the effects of the Planets in each [sign] / has to observe the common stars / at which place they are located in our time / and has to combine the nature of the stars with the nature of the Planets / There are as well some stars on the outside of the zodiac towards the north / and some of them towards the south / which Ptolemy has compared to some animals or creatures / and his opinion is as follows. If there is a solar or lunar eclipse / and an evil Planet is with them / which makes people die / then the ones will die / after which the stars are formed / be it human / animal / bird or fish etc.

---

[520] *Zalkunst*, from *Zahlenkunst*, literally "the art of numbers", or "arithmetic"

[521] *Stelle fixe*

and his opinion is that in those a similar illness will develop / and there are as well some stars in the zodiac / which are quite large / as if they were Planets / and some are small / and some are of average size. It should be known as well / that the stars which are red / are of Mars' nature and hot / and the ones that are white / they are of Saturn's nature / and are cold. One should know as well / that all stars are glinting and flickering[522] / only Planets do not glint or flicker.

On the seventh heaven to list them / stands Saturn / on the sixth / Jupiter on the fifth / Mars on the fourth / the[523] [---] and on the third Venus / on the other Mercury / and Luna on the first / and these heavens are all revolving daily with the ix. heaven / but Motus Raptus the Planets move according to their own motion against the ix. heaven / one faster than the other.

Of the Epicycle

Each Planet has a small circle which is called epicycle[524] / only the Sun has no epicycle / and these epicycles are divided into xii. signs too / and each sign into xxx. degrees / and the signs on the epicycle are called argumentum in auge / this is on the uppermost part of the epicycle / and one can see from it / where the Planet is standing in its epicycle. The centre of the epicycle is called Centrum epicicli / which is always moving in the same way on the zodiac in the Sun's path / and it is called deferent[525] of the Planets / but the Planet is moving along the epicycle / and at some point it is standing in its epicycle / at some point it is below / then it is rising / then it is setting / and realizing this / if there is neither sign nor degree in the

---

[522] *zwitzern* Middle High German for *zittern, flimmern*, "to glimmer", or "to flicker".

[523] The word "Sun" is missing in the text.

[524] *epiciclus*

[525] *mittellauf*

argument[526] / then the Planet is in [its] auge[527] / this is on the uppermost part of its epicycle[528] / but if there are six signs and no degree in the argument / so the Planet is on the lowest point of its epicycle / and it is called opposite [its] auge[529] / but if there are three signs in the argument / so the Planet is next to the epicycle and is declining / but if there are nine signs in the argument / so the Planet is next to the epicycle and is rising. Each Planet declining in its epicycle is turned towards rising / and if it is rising it is turned towards setting / The Moon is not doing the same / when he declines / he is turned towards setting / and if he rises / he is turned towards rising. The deferent[530] of a Planet / this is the equal motion of the centre of its epicycle along the Sun's path on the zodiac / but the irregular motion[531] or transverse movement[532] of the Planet / is the movement of the Planet / up or down / forwards or backwards on the epicycle.[533]

Of the Movement of the Planets against the Firmament

The movement of the Sun in one day is sixty minutes / those sixty make one movement[534] / and sixty minutes make one hour / twenty four of them make one day / and eight seconds / against the movement of the firmament.

---

[526] *argumento*

[527] From the Latin *augeo*, "increase" or "augment".

[528] That is the Apogee, the furthest point from the centre of the Earth.

[529] *oppositum augis*

[530] *mittellauf*

[531] *irgang*

[532] Reading *gewerelauff*, "transverse movement".

[533] I have included an explanatory graphic in Appendix B.

[534] *momentum*

The movement of the Sun in one year [which] is in 365. days is 359. degrees and xlv. minutes.

The movement of the epicycle of the Moon towards rising in one day is xiii. degrees / and ten minutes / this movement will be completed in xxix. days and viiii. hours.

The movement of the epicycle of Saturn towards rising in one day is two minutes / in one solar year it is twelve degrees / and thirteen minutes / this movement will be completed in thirty years / after common calculation.

The movement of the epicycle of Jupiter towards rising in one day is four minutes / in one solar year it is thirty degrees and twenty minutes / and thirteen minutes / this movement will be completed in twelve years.

The movement of the epicycle of Mars towards rising in one day is xxxi. minutes / in one solar year it is xix. degrees / and xvi. minutes / this movement will be completed in two years.

The movement of the epicycle of Venus towards rising in one day is lix. minutes / in one solar year it is xii degrees[535] / and xlv. minutes / this movement will be completed in one year.

The movement of the epicycle of Mercury towards rising in one day is lix. minutes / in one solar year it is twelve degrees[536] / and xlv. minutes / this movement will be completed in one year / after common number.

Note / epicycle is the circle every Planet is rising along towards the rising of heaven / and once it is on the uppermost point of the circle / it moves in its centre / which is a plane in the middle. And therefore the uppermost part of the so called circle is called epicycle / as said before / The Earth has 52200. stadia / 315000. miles / It is as well said / that [the size of] the Sun is 166. times the Earth / therefore to whom is counting correctly / she is 5224000.

---

[535] *zeichen* ("sign"), reading "degree" for "sign"

[536] Ibid.

miles / It is as well said / that the Moon has a size of 870. miles / and half a pert of a mile / and one eighth or one stadium / and half a stadium / and 81 paces[537] / and iii. feet[538] / and one finger / and nearly one grain of barley / this will be known through the numbers of the art of calculating[539] / which is called arithmetic / to one dot no more and no less / like the miles of the other Planets / it is studiously observed.

Note / each degree of the sign bearer / which is called zodiac / has 1000. times 1000. and 100. times and 40. times to one time 1000.72. miles / It is as well said that the motion of the Moon / against the movement of the firmament / or the eighth heaven / is xiii. degrees and x. minutes / of the parts of the circle called zodiac / therefore the Moon in his own movement against rising in each natural day moves 10. times 1000. times / 4. times 1000. times 800. times 1000. times / and 5000. and 259. miles. The movement of the Sun spreads [over] all days with its movement / against the firmament nearly 1000. times 1000. and 100. times and 40.times for once times 1000. and 62 miles / because one degree of the circle [of the] zodiac includes as much / as has been said before.

And the Sun passes one degree nearly every day / or fifty nine minutes and eight seconds / as mentioned before / and as it is concerning the width of the motion of the Sun and the Moon / therefore everybody who is knowledgeable in the art of arithmetic / [may] calculate / and find all the miles of all the other Planets.

Of the four Parts of Heaven

Heaven is separated into four parts / one is east[540] / the other west[541] / the third south[542] / the fourth north[543] / East is where the Sun rises in the

---

[537] *schrit*

[538] *füß*

[539] *Rechenkunst*

[540] *uffgang*

morning / west is where she sets in the evening / the south[544] is where she stays at noon / and north[545] where she is at midnight / Heaven is divided into two other parts / a line or circle in heaven along the middle of the Earth / and this circle is stretching from the orient to the occident / and back to the orient / this circle is called equinoctial line[546] / when the Sun is on this line day and night are of equal length / this line separates the zodiac into two parts / so that there are six signs on the other side of the line / they are called southerly[547] / and there are six signs on this side of the line too / they are called northerly[548] / three of them are rising / those are / Aries / Taurus / Gemini / and three are setting which are / Cancer / Leo / Virgo / [Of] the six towards south three are setting too which are / Libra / Scorpio / Sagittarius / and three are rising / Capricorn / Aquarius / Pisces.

Ptolemy writes in the book called *Script.* when the Sun moves into Aries / spring begins / and [it] lasts until the Sun is moving into Cancer / and summer begins / and lasts until the Sun moves into Libra / and then autumn begins / and [it] lasts until the Sun moves into Capricorn / then winter begins / and lasts until the Sun is moving into Aries again.

Of the Movement of the Heavens and Planets

---

[541] *nidergang*

[542] *mittag*

[543] *midnacht*

[544] *meridies mittag*

[545] *Cardo mittnacht*

[546] *linea equinoctialis*

[547] *mittäglich*

[548] *mitternächtlich*

Theodosius / Ambrosius / and master Johannes de Sacrobosco[549] in his sphere[550] / in the book / which he extracted from other books / Of the movement of the heavens / and stars / and Planets too / which are called irregular stars[551] / because their motion is different from the rising or the setting of the Sun or the Moon / therefore it may lead astray to look at them / because their movement is across the world / meaning / that the same Planets now rise here / now there / where they are setting / and move against the motion of the firmament.

Division of the Earth[552]

The Earth is divided into four parts / as if a line would run straight through the Earth / from dawn[553] to dusk[554] / and the other line runs from the south[555] to the north[556] / those two lines are called the two Coluri[557] [note in left margin: Coluri. Brentzreiffe][558] / the lines which divide the Earth into four parts / are called as follows. Equinoctial towards the north / one

---

[549] *Johannes der Engellender von Sacrobusto*

[550] His work *On the Sphere,* published in ca. 1220

[551] *Irresternen,* originally from Middle High German *irre-stern*, "a comet".

[552] *Ertrich,* from Old High German *ërdrîchi,* "earth" as compared to "heaven".

[553] *Aufgang*

[554] *Nidergang*

[555] *mittag*

[556] *Norwegen*

[557] From the Latin *colura,* "two circles" through equinoctial and solstitial points perpendicular at the poles.

[558] Literally "the (two) burning circles", from *brennen,* "to burn" and *reif*, an old German word for "ring" or "circle".

seventh of the Earth / they are called vii. climates[559] / One should know what the masters write / that below these lines / and at the line which is called Equinoctial / nobody can live there because of too much heat / and this line is also called the hot zone[560] / and at the same time nobody wants to live where the seven climates are ending below the northern pole[561] or nearby because of the great cold / But in between the climate is divided into seven / as is written below.

The seven Climates

The first climate begins in India / and exists along the line which is called equinoctial from the east towards the west / and the width of this climate is facing towards the north / and so are all the other climates / and in this climate the day is according to rough calculations xiii. hours at its longest / But in the centre of the climate the day is a little bit longer / Take note that below the line which is called equinoctial the day is longest / xii. hours / and the beginning of the first climate is one hour away from the line / Saturn belongs to this climate and the ii. signs Capricorn and Aquarius / in this climate are many castles / places and towns / we don't know about / and therefore we leave them alone.

The other climate begins in the east[562] and continues to extend into the direction of the west[563] too / and the beginning of its width / is where the first climate ends / and there the length of the day is xiii. hours / and half an hour / But in its centre it is longer / The Planet Jupiter belongs to this

---

[559] *Climata*

[560] *Torida zona,* from the Latin *torridus,* "parched", "scorched", "hot" or "torrid".

[561] *polo artico*

[562] *uffgang*

[563] *Nidergang*

climate / and the ii. signs Sagittarius and Pisces / in this climate are placed Egypt and Ethiopia[564] / and borders onto Alexandria.

The third climate begins in the east and extends through India / and through Greece / Sicily and Poland[565] / and continues towards the west / The Planet Mars belongs to this climate / and the ii. signs Aries and Scorpio / this climate extends from where the other one ends / and the longest day is fourteen hours / but in the centre of the climate it is a little bit longer.

The fourth climate begins in the east and extends towards the west / and begins at the width where the third climate ends / and there the longest day is xiiii. hours and half an hour / but in the centre of this climate it is a little bit longer / Rome is situated in this climate / and Campania and Tuscany[566] and other countries and cities / The Sun and the sign of Leo belong to this sign.[567]

The fifth climate extends between the east and the west / and its width begins / where the width of the fourth climate ends / and the longest day is xv. hours / but in the centre of the climate it is a little bit longer / In this climate lies Lombardy[568] / Bolognia[569] / and Milan / and many other places up to Spain / Venus is this climate's Planet and these two signs / Taurus and Libra.

The sixth climate extends in length from the east towards the west / and in its width it begins / where the fifth ends / and the day is xv. hours long and

---

[564] *Morenland*

[565] *Bulle*

[566] *Tuschan*

[567] Printer's mistake for "climate".

[568] *Lamparten* Middle High German for *Lombardei*.

[569] *Bononia,* keltic name of Bolognia.

half an hour / and the climate extends through the Swiss mountains down into Germany / In this climate lie Venice / Hungary / Austria and France / this climate belongs to Mercury / and the two signs Gemini and Virgo.

The seventh climate extends in length from the east towards the west / and in width it extends towards the north until the end / this climate begins where the sixth ends / and the longest day lasts xvi. hours / and in its centre it is longer / but at the end it is very long / In this climate there are many countries and many pleasant towns and castles / like Strasbourg / Mainz and Cologne / [Proband?]570 and England / Franconia / Thuringia / Hesse / and many other countries / towns and castles / which I cannot all name / the Moon and the sign of Cancer belong to this climate / Now you have the sign[s] of the seven climates to a rough account / as they are separated by most of the masters.

The masters say as well / whoever wants to know which Planet rules in each country / town / village / or castle / should take heed of the manners of the people in the region / and which Planet's nature they are most similar to / this Planet will have its greatest influence in the region. Although the climates are now separated in a way / that the Sun and Leo have power over the country of the Romans / Ptolemy has separated the three fire signs into three regions / and says that Aries is [ruling] over the land of the Romans / and over Tuscany571 and Lombardy572 / so Leo is [ruling] over Hungary / Bohemia / Prussia and Germany / and Sagittarius is [ruling] over France / Spain / Portugal / Scotland and England / and his opinion is as well / when a Solar or Lunar eclipse / or a comet / or a great conjunction of the high Planets is in one of the three signs / so the judgement / if it is good or bad / goes into the country / which the sign belongs to.

---

570 So far I have not been able to locate this place.

571 *Tuschan*

572 *Lamparten*

[The] hemisphere is the whole heaven visible over the mountain / or above the land of each country. [The] horizon[573] is only the circle on the Earth / it is where the light of heaven touches the Earth. [The] zenith is the part of heaven which is above our heads / When the Sun is rising and touches the horizon in the east[574] the day begins and lasts until the Sun moves below the horizon in the west[575] / and this is called night / and therefore the Sun divides heaven into two parts / which is into day and into night / the day is warm and dry / the night cold and moist / We have said enough of this.

Sphere of the Winds

Of the four Winds and their twelve Corners

The Sphere of the Winds / shows when Mars reigns because then wind and clouds are coming from the south[576] / But if Jupiter reigns / they come from the north / and if Saturn reigns they come from the east / north east / and from north / north east / and so forth.

The four Regions or Heavens

There are quatuor regionis which are four regions or countries / the first country is called orient[577] / and this is the land or place which is situated in front of mountains / which are radiated by the rising early morning Sun / and the region is warm and dry. The other land is called occident[578] / and this is the land or region / which is placed in front of mountains which are

---

[573] *Orizon*

[574] *Aufgang*

[575] *Nidergang*

[576] *mittag*

[577] *Morgenland*

[578] *Abendland*

radiated by the setting evening Sun / and this [region] is cold and wet. The third region is the land to the south[579] / and there the mountains are facing south[580] / and [it] is warm and moist / the fourth region is the land of the north[581] / and [this] is the country where the mountains are facing north.[582]

---

[579] *Mittagland*

[580] *mittag*

[581] *Mitnachtland*

[582] *norwegen*

Appendix A

In the chapter *Of the Complexion of the Twelve Signs and Planets*, the author mentions the fact that there were different tables of terms in existence. He is probably referring to the Chaldean table, the Hindu one or the one given by Ptolemy in his *Tetrabiblos*. Although stating his preference for the Egyptian Terms, he does not provide the all important table. Al Biruni is of the opinion that only the Egyptian and Ptolemaic terms would be worth discussing. The following graphics show the Tables of the Egyptian Terms after Al Biruni[583] and Firmicus Maternus[584] which are differing slightly.

♈	♃ 6	♀ 12	☿ 20	♂ 25	♄ 30
♉	♀ 8	☿ 14	♃ 22	♄ 27	♂ 30
♊	☿ 6	♃ 12	♀ 17	♂ 24	♄ 30
♋	♂ 7	♀ 13	☿ 19	♃ 26	♄ 30
♌	♃ 6	♀ 11	♄ 18	☿ 24	♂ 30

---

[583] Al Biruni: *The Book of Instructions in the Elements of the Art of Astrology*, Astrology Classics, 2006.

[584] Maternus, Firmicus: *Matheseos Libri VIII*, Astrology Classics, 2005.

♍	☿ 7	♀ 17	♃ 21	♂ 28	♄ 30
♎	♄ 6	☿ 14	♃ 21	♀ 28	♂ 30
♏	♂ 7	♀ 11	☿ 19	♃ 24	♄ 30
♐	♃ 12	♀ 17	☿ 21	♄ 26	♂ 30
♑	☿ 7	♃ 14	♀ 22	♄ 26	♂ 30
♒	☿ 7	♀ 13	♃ 20	♂ 25	♄ 30
♓	♀ 12	♃ 16	☿ 19	♂ 28	♄ 30

(Egyptian Terms after Al Biruni)

♈	♃ 6	♀ 12	☿ 20	♂ 25	♄ 30
♉	♀ 8	☿ 14	♃ 22	♄ 27	♂ 30
♊	☿ 6	♃ 12	♀ 18	♂ 24	♄ 30
♋	♂ 7	♀ 13	☿ 20	♃ 27	♄ 30
♌	♃ 6	♀ 11	♄ 18	☿ 24	♂ 30
♍	☿ 7	♀ 17	♃ 21	♂ 28	♄ 30
♎	♄ 6	☿ 14	♃ 21	♀ 28	♂ 30
♏	♂ 7	♀ 11	☿ 19	♃ 24	♄ 30
♐	♃ 12	♀ 17	☿ 23	♄ 27	♂ 30

♑	☿ 7	♃ 14	♀ 22	♄ 26	♂ 30
♒	☿ 7	♀ 13	♃ 20	♂ 25	♄ 30
♓	♀ 12	♃ 16	☿ 19	♂ 28	♄ 30

(Egyptian Terms after Firmicus Maternus)

Appendix B

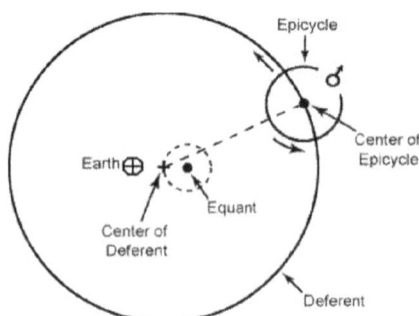

The diagram above may help to understand the difficult chapters *On the Sphere* and *Another Explanation of the Spheres and Circles of Heaven.* It shows the Earth as the centre of the universe and Mars, representing the Planets, which is travelling counter clockwise on its epicycle. The whole epicycle moves counter-clockwise in a circle, called deferent, with its centre labelled **+**. The centre of the Earth is offset from the centre of the deferent, which, in extremis, leads to a position of the Planet furthest apart from the Earth. This is called "argumentum in auge" or apogee of the Planet. Another point discussed in the text is the "argument". Here the distance of a Planet from the apogee (auge) of its epicycle is measured. A reoccurring problem is the fact that the apogee can be measured either from the centre of the Earth or the centre of the equant (see diagram). The difference between both of these measurements is called the equation of the argument.

The text mentions the tables of the Planet's deferents but does not provide them. To give an example of these tables, the following is a reproduction of the tables of Saturn's deferent for the years between 1500 and 1600 AD and the table for the month, days, hours and minutes of Saturn's deferent from Rensberger's *Astronomia Teutsch*.[585]

Table of Saturn's Deferent for the Years 1500 to 1600

	S.	D.	M.		S.	D.	M.		S.	D.	M.		S.	D.	M
1500	2	6	6	28	1	18	14	57	1	1	15	84	0	13	
1	2	18	20	29	2	0	55	57	1	13	29	85	0	26	
2	3	0	34	1530	2	13	8	58	1	25	42	86	1	8	
3	3	12	47	31	2	25	22	59	2	7	56	87	1	20	
4	3	25	3	32	3	7	37	1560	2	20	11	88	2	2	
5	4	7	16	33	3	19	51	61	3	2	25	89	2	17	
6	4	19	30	34	4	2	4	62	3	14	39	1590	2	27	
7	5	1	44	35	4	14	18	63	3	26	52	91	3	9	
8	5	13	59	36	4	26	34	64	4	9	8	92	3	21	
9	5	26	13	37	5	8	47	65	4	21	21	93	4	3	
1510	6	8	27	38	5	21	1	66	5	3	35	94	4	16	
11	6	20	40	39	6	3	4	67	5	15	49	95	4	28	
12	7	2	56	1540	6	15	30	68	5	28	4	96	5	10	
13	7	15	9	41	6	27	43	69	6	10	18	97	5	22	
14	7	27	23	42	7	9	57	1570	6	22	31	98	5	5	

---

[585] Rensberger, Nicolaus: *Astronomia teutsch dergleichen vormals nye in Druck aufzgangen*, Augspurg, 1569.

A German Stargazer's Book of Astrology

15	8	9	37	43	7	22	10	71	7	4	45	99	6	17	17
16	8	21	52	44	8	4	16	72	7	17	1	1600	6	29	35
17	9	4	6	45	8	16	40	73	7	29	14				
18	9	16	19	46	8	28	53	74	8	11	28				
19	9	28	33	47	9	11	7	75	8	23	41				
1520	10	10	48	48	9	23	22	76	9	5	57				
21	10	23	2	49	10	5	36	77	9	18	1				
22	11	5	15	1550	10	17	50	78	10	0	24				
23	11	17	29	51	11	0	3	79	10	12	38				
24	11	29	45	52	11	12	19	1580	10	24	53				
25	0	11	58	53	11	24	32	81	11	7	6				
26	0	24	12	54	0	6	46	82	11	19	20				
27	1	6	25	55	0	19	0	83	0	1	34				

A German Stargazer's Book of Astrology

Table of Saturn's deferent in month, days, hours and minutes:

Ordinary Year	S.	D.	M.	Day	D.	M.	Hour:	D.	M.
January	0	1	2	1	0	2	1	0	0
February	0	1	58	2	0	4	2	0	0
March	0	3	0	3	0	6	3	0	0
April	0	4	1	4	0	8	4	0	0
May	0	5	3	5	0	10	5	0	0
June	0	6	3	6	0	12	6	0	0
July	0	7	6	7	0	14	7	0	0
August	0	8	8	8	0	16	8	0	0
September	0	9	8	9	0	18	9	0	0
October	0	10	11	10	0	20	10	0	0
November	0	11	11	11	0	22	11	0	0
December	0	12	13	12	0	24	12	0	1
				13	0	26	13	0	1
				14	0	28	14	0	1
				15	0	30	15	0	1
				16	0	32	16	0	1
Leap year				17	0	34	17	0	1
				18	0	36	18	0	1
January	0	1	2	19	0	38	19	0	1

February	0	2	0	20	0	40	20	0	1
March	0	3	2	21	0	42	21	0	1
April	0	4	3	22	0	44	22	0	1
May	0	5	5	23	0	46	23	0	1
June	0	6	5	24	0	48	24	0	2
July	0	7	8	25	0	50	25	0	2
August	0	8	10	26	0	52	26	0	2
September	0	9	10	27	0	54	27	0	2
October	0	10	12	28	0	56	28	0	2
November	0	11	13	29	0	58	29	0	2
December	0	12	15	30	0	0	30	0	2

Rensberger provides an example for a person being born on the 8th of January 1529 at 07:53. His calculation of the deferent of Saturn is shown below.

	Degree	Hour	Minute
1528	1	18	41
Month 0	0	0	0
Day 8	0	0	16
Hour 7	0	0	0
Minute 53	0	0	0
----------	----------	----------	----------
Deferent ♄	1	18	57

Index

Abenragel 13, 150
Actophylax 74
Albumasar 12, 13, 118, 144, 163
Alchindus 14, 162, 164, 165, 166, 167
Alferas 81
Alfraganus 14, 17, 217, 219
Andromeda 22, 33, 72, 81, 82, 202
Anticanis 73, 96
Aquarius 33, 56, 68, 71, 72, 79, 85, 87, 88, 89, 93, 96, 99, 107, 109, 113, 118, 135, 143, 149, 157, 169, 172, 174, 175, 176, 180, 185, 218, 226, 228
Arctophilax 74, 93
Arctura 74
Arcturus 21, 73, 78, 93, 187, 198
Argo 23, 33, 72, 91, 184, 188, 190, 203
Aries 17, 18, 29, 34, 54, 57, 58, 71, 72, 75, 80, 81, 82, 83, 86, 89, 101, 107, 109, 110, 113, 115, 116, 117, 118, 119, 120, 135, 142, 144, 157, 168, 169, 171, 172, 175, 177, 190, 213, 218, 220, 225, 226, 228, 230
Astronomy 210
Astronothus 72, 92

Balena 87
Banner 98
Boetes 72, 78
Brachmon 196
Butzahan 15, 142, 143, 147

Cancer 34, 55, 61, 62, 71, 72, 90, 91, 92, 93, 97, 109, 111, 113, 115, 118, 119, 135, 143, 146, 165, 168, 169, 171, 173, 175, 176, 179, 183, 218, 225, 226, 229
Canis 23, 24, 35, 39, 72, 90, 91, 96, 184, 194
Capricorn 36, 56, 58, 67, 68, 71, 72, 81, 84, 85, 87, 89, 92, 93, 96, 97, 99, 109, 113, 118, 119, 135, 142, 149, 157, 169, 172, 174, 175, 177, 184, 218, 226, 228
Cardanus 15
Cassiopeia 21, 36, 72, 80, 205
Centaurus 23, 36, 72, 92, 94, 95, 194, 203, 205
Centres of the Moon 181
Cepheus 21, 36, 79, 80, 198
Cetus 22, 37, 72, 87, 88, 202
Change of the Air 177
Charioteer 78, 193, 194, 195, 204, 209
Cignus 85
Climates 227
Clotha 84
Comets 142
Complexion 107
Conjunctions 127
Corona 20, 37, 76, 183

Daemon Meridianus 92

Delphinus 23, 72, 89, 158
Dignities 112
Drill 97

Eclipses 137
Elevation 123
Epicycle 221
Equus Vespertinus 81
Eridanus 23, 72, 88
Erndmon 200
Eugonasin 75

Fall 113
Fixed Stars 14, 19, 20, 49, 72, 73, 219

Gallina 84
Gemini 38, 47, 55, 60, 61, 71, 72, 78, 91, 97, 107, 109, 115, 118, 135, 140, 143, 145, 157, 160, 168, 171, 173, 187, 218, 225, 229
Great Bear 20, 72, 73, 74, 184, 187, 188, 189, 190, 195, 196, 198, 202, 203, 205, 206, 209

Hali 13, 118, 150, 176
Hartmon 183
Heavenly Signs 54
Herbstmon 202
Hercules 20, 72, 75, 76
Hewmon 198
Hornung 186
Hydra 24, 73, 95, 96, 187

Joculato 88

Joy 113
Jupiter 100
Leo 35, 39, 55, 62, 63, 71, 72, 90, 91, 95, 98, 102, 107, 109, 113, 115, 117, 142, 146, 157, 168, 171, 173, 175, 176, 184, 199, 218, 225, 229, 230
Lepus 23, 39, 72, 91, 207
Libra 30, 40, 55, 65, 71, 72, 76, 78, 82, 94, 95, 107, 109, 110, 113, 115, 118, 119, 120, 135, 143, 147, 157, 169, 171, 174, 177, 191, 218, 225, 226, 229
Little Bear 20, 72, 74, 75
Lord of the Year 117
Lucina 105
Lyra 22, 39, 40, 43, 72, 84, 85, 86, 87, 184, 185, 186, 193, 194, 195, 200, 201, 205, 206, 207

Macrobius 15
Mars 100
Mercury 103
Messahalla 16, 118
Month of Christ 208
Moon 104

Navis 91, 188

Ophiuchus 42, 77, 197
Orion 23, 42, 72, 88, 89, 90, 186, 196, 197, 198, 199, 200, 201, 205, 206, 207, 208, 209

Parts of Heaven 225
Pegasus 21, 43, 72, 81, 82, 189, 190, 202, 203
Perpetual Calendar 183
Perseus 22, 72, 82, 83, 193
Pisces 18, 43, 56, 64, 69, 71, 72, 80, 81, 83, 86, 88, 93, 100, 109, 113, 118, 143, 150, 165, 169, 172, 174, 175, 180, 187, 190, 218, 220, 226, 228
Piscis magnus 93
Planetary aspects 115
Planetary Portals 181
Planetary Strength 134
Polus Arcticus 74
Prokyon 96
Ptolemy 15, 16, 18, 28, 74, 77, 78, 80, 82, 83, 84, 85, 86, 87, 88, 89, 90, 91, 93, 94, 95, 96, 118, 137, 139, 140, 151, 153, 157, 158, 162, 163, 164, 165, 166, 183, 209, 217, 220, 226, 230, 232
Puteus 72, 94

Revolutions 116

Sacrarius 94
Sacrobosco 17, 219, 226
Sagittarius 44, 56, 64, 66, 67, 71, 72, 73, 75, 85, 89, 92, 97, 107, 109, 113, 118, 142, 148, 157, 169, 171, 174, 175, 187, 218, 225, 228, 230
Saturn 99
Scorpio 34, 44, 56, 65, 66, 71, 72, 75, 77, 92, 94, 101, 109, 113, 117, 136, 143, 148, 157, 165, 169, 171, 174, 175, 180, 205, 218, 225, 228
Seasons of the year 170
Serpentarius 72, 77, 197
Signs and Images 17
Sirion 90
Spheres of Heaven 210
Sun 101

Taurus 18, 45, 54, 58, 59, 71, 72, 78, 79, 82, 83, 84, 87, 89, 91, 103, 109, 113, 117, 142, 145, 157, 168, 171, 173, 175, 177, 192, 218, 220, 225, 229
Testudo 92
Triangulus 83

Ursa Minor 74, 78

Venus 102
Virgo 30, 47, 55, 63, 64, 71, 72, 76, 78, 82, 95, 98, 109, 113, 118, 140, 142, 147, 157, 158, 169, 171, 174, 187, 218, 225, 229
Vultur cadens 86
Vultur volans 86

Weather 168
Wine Month 204
Winter Month 205

Ingram Content Group UK Ltd.
Milton Keynes UK
UKHW031831220523
422165UK00009B/167